MW00474845

Curriculum-Based Assessment for Instructional Design

The Guilford Practical Intervention in the Schools Series

Kenneth W. Merrell, Founding Editor
T. Chris Riley-Tillman, Series Editor

www.guilford.com/practical

This series presents the most reader-friendly resources available in key areas of evidence-based practice in school settings. Practitioners will find trustworthy guides on effective behavioral, mental health, and academic interventions, and assessment and measurement approaches. Covering all aspects of planning, implementing, and evaluating high-quality services for students, books in the series are carefully crafted for everyday utility. Features include ready-to-use reproducibles, lay-flat binding to facilitate photocopying, appealing visual elements, and an oversized format. Recent titles have companion Web pages where purchasers can download and print the reproducible materials.

Recent Volumes

RTI Applications, Volume 1: Academic and Behavioral Interventions
Matthew K. Burns, T. Chris Riley-Tillman, and Amanda M. VanDerHeyden

Coaching Students with Executive Skills Deficits
Peg Dawson and Richard Guare

Enhancing Instructional Problem Solving:
An Efficient System for Assisting Struggling Learners
John C. Begeny, Ann C. Schulte, and Kent Johnson

Clinical Interviews for Children and Adolescents, Second Edition:
Assessment to Intervention
Stephanie H. McConaughy

RTI Team Building: Effective Collaboration and Data-Based Decision Making
Kelly Broxterman and Angela J. Whalen

RTI Applications, Volume 2: Assessment, Analysis, and Decision Making
T. Chris Riley-Tillman, Matthew K. Burns, and Kimberly Gibbons

Daily Behavior Report Cards: An Evidence-Based System of Assessment and Intervention
Robert J. Volpe and Gregory A. Fabiano

Assessing Intelligence in Children and Adolescents:
A Practical Guide
John H. Kranzler and Randy G. Floyd

The RTI Approach to Evaluating Learning Disabilities
Joseph F. Kovaleski, Amanda M. VanDerHeyden, and Edward S. Shapiro

Resilient Classrooms, Second Edition: Creating Healthy Environments for Learning
Beth Doll, Katherine Brehm, and Steven Zucker

The ABCs of Curriculum-Based Evaluation: A Practical Guide
to Effective Decision Making
John L. Hosp, Michelle K. Hosp, Kenneth W. Howell, and Randy Allison

Curriculum-Based Assessment for Instructional Design:
Using Data to Individualize Instruction
Matthew K. Burns and David C. Parker

Curriculum-Based Assessment for Instructional Design

Using Data to Individualize Instruction

MATTHEW K. BURNS
DAVID C. PARKER

Foreword by James A. Tucker

THE GUILFORD PRESS
New York   London

© 2014 The Guilford Press
A Division of Guilford Publications, Inc.
72 Spring Street, New York, NY 10012
www.guilford.com

All rights reserved

Except as indicated, no part of this book may be reproduced, translated, stored in a retrieval
system, or transmitted, in any form or by any means, electronic, mechanical, photocopying,
microfilming, recording, or otherwise, without written permission from the publisher.

Printed in the United States of America

This book is printed on acid-free paper.

Last digit is print number: 9   8   7   6   5   4   3   2   1

LIMITED PHOTOCOPY LICENSE

These materials are intended for use only by qualified professionals.

The publisher grants to individual purchasers of this book nonassignable permission to
reproduce all materials for which photocopying permission is specifically granted in a
footnote. This license is limited to you, the individual purchaser, for personal use or use with
individual students. This license does not grant the right to reproduce these materials for
resale, redistribution, electronic display, or any other purposes (including but not limited to
books, pamphlets, articles, video- or audiotapes, blogs, file-sharing sites, Internet or intranet
sites, and handouts or slides for lectures, workshops, or webinars, whether or not a fee is
charged). Permission to reproduce these materials for these and any other purposes must be
obtained in writing from the Permissions Department of Guilford Publications.

Library of Congress Cataloging-in-Publication Data

Burns, Matthew K.
   Curriculum-based assessment for instructional design : using data to individualize instruction /
Matthew K. Burns, David C. Parker.
      pages cm.—(The Guilford practical intervention in the schools series)
   Includes bibliographical references and index.
   ISBN 978-1-4625-1440-3 (pbk.)
   1. Individualized instruction.   2. Curriculum-based assessment.   I. Parker, David C.,
1983–   II. Title.
   LB1031.B868 2014
   371.394—dc23

                                                                    2013038805

*This book is dedicated first and foremost to the children
with whom we have worked and from whom we learned
so much. Matthew Burns also dedicates this book to
the NATSCI 125 professor at Michigan State University who,
in the spring of 1987, told him that he would never amount
to anything because of his bad handwriting.
While studying in Spain, David Parker received similar
inspiration from a Spanish literature professor.
He also dedicates this book to the skilled, passionate educators
who embrace new, effective solutions to help all students
reach their learning potential.*

About the Authors

Matthew K. Burns, PhD, is Professor of Educational Psychology, Coordinator of the School Psychology Program, and Co-Director of the Minnesota Center for Reading Research at the University of Minnesota. He has published over 150 articles and book chapters and 10 books, including *Evaluating Educational Interventions*; *RTI Applications, Volume 1: Academic and Behavioral Interventions*; and *RTI Applications, Volume 2: Assessment, Analysis, and Decision Making*. Dr. Burns is the Editor of *School Psychology Review*.

David C. Parker, PhD, is Research Director at ServeMinnesota, the state commission tasked with administering Americorps programming in Minnesota. ServeMinnesota operates Minnesota Reading Corps and Math Corps, which apply research-based practices in assessment and intervention within and beyond Minnesota schools in order to support at-risk learners. Dr. Parker has published multiple articles and chapters on instructionally relevant assessment and intervention, and has worked as a school psychologist and school psychology trainer.

Foreword

Assessment always should be based in the curriculum and the curriculum always should be aligned with assessment. *Authentic assessment* is a term that has emerged to address this alignment (Ellis, 2005). The best way to accomplish authentic assessment is to integrate the assessment into the learning experience as a continuous process, which is very different from the standardized assessment process mandated by most states.

In the mid-1970s, educators began to note the lack of correlation between standardized, norm-referenced measures and the curricular materials being used. Such alignment ceased to be feasible when the standard curriculum began to exceed the material, the skills, or both that could be assessed efficiently and effectively. It was only a matter of time until this matter began to appear in the literature (Jenkins & Pany, 1978; Mercer & Ysseldyke, 1977), and it was not surprising that a number of educators began to provide a way to return to data-based instruction (Durkin, 1984; Gickling & Havertape, 1981; Samuels, 1984). That is what curriculum-based assessment for instructional design (CBA-ID) is all about. But I am getting somewhat ahead of the story. A review of the history of CBA-ID is necessary for an understanding of its basic design and intent.

Sometimes terms arise because they are self-evident and obvious. This was not so in the case of curriculum-based assessment. In 1980, members of the Advisory Board of the School Psychology Training Project of the University of Minnesota asked me to compile a collection of practical approaches to assessment that were alternatives to standardized testing. The result, *Non-Test-Based Assessment*, was published by the University of Minnesota the following year (Tucker, 1981).

The publication consisted of three training modules for school psychologists. The first module, "Observation-Based Assessment," comes from Vance and Marian Hall (1981). The module contains practical and effective techniques for observing and recording behavior and then translating those observations into interventions, which sets up the cycle of continuously recorded observations using the same simple techniques. The Halls developed their methods from the perspective of applied behavior analysis, a field to which they contributed heavily.

Edward Gickling developed the second module. At that time, Gickling was a faculty member at the University of Tennessee, Knoxville. His material is based in part on research about a technique that used the work that the student was assigned as the basis for assessment in an ongoing evaluation of progress. This technique assured that the student's assigned work was at an instructional level based on the assessment of the student's existing knowledge and skills (Gickling & Armstrong, 1978).

The third module was developed by Robert Audette, then commissioner of Special Education for the Massachusetts Department of Education. Audette proposed the idea of developing a method of interviewing the student, the teacher, and the parent, and then finding congruence among the responses of all three in order to develop an understanding of what objectives to set as well as how to evaluate whether or not those objectives were met.

So, we had an observation-of-behavior module, a measure-of-ongoing-achievement module, and an interview-based module. Alan Coulter assisted me in the depiction of these modules. As he and I considered how to present the three modules, we determined that it would be useful to give the titles parallel construction. The first module was in place with the descriptive title "Observation-Based Assessment" (Hall & Hall, 1981). The name of the third module fell naturally and quickly into place as "Interview-Based Assessment" (Audette & Coulter, 1981).

That left the Gickling module. We labored over the words and eventually concluded that what was being assessed was the student's progress in the curriculum. Thus "Curriculum-Based Assessment" (CBA) came to be (Gickling & Havertape, 1981). If the proof of a concept is in its staying power, this concept was, and still is, valid. But therein lies the germ of a problem that quickly arose. Once named, the concept gained momentum because of its demonstrated effectiveness, and its popularity seemed to attract the association of other assessments that were not in harmony with the conceptual framework from which CBA emerged. It became necessary, therefore, to define more specifically what that framework looked like.

In 1985, a special issue of *Exceptional Children* was dedicated to examining CBA, and we inadvertently further confused the description of CBA because the definitional elements of CBA were so varied. However, the basic concept was clearly presented in that publication: "Curriculum-based assessment (CBA) is the ultimate in 'teaching the test,' because the materials used to assess progress are *always* drawn directly from the course of study" (Tucker, 1985, p. 200). Furthermore, as defined initially, "in curriculum-based assessment the essential measure of success in education is the student's progress *in the curriculum* of the local school" (p. 199). This form of assessment stood in stark contrast to obtaining performance data from an alternate curriculum or from some standardized-item pool of controlled instructional objectives. This is not to say, however, that CBA provided something new in effective instruction.

As a concept, CBA is timeless. CBA is simply old-fashioned data-based instructional management reincarnated. I say "reincarnated" because the skills had largely died out and were no longer in common practice in classroom instruction. I believe that the demise of these skills was aided significantly—if not caused—by the dramatic rise in the use of standardized tests to measure student achievement. Gradually, educators lost contact with the direct relationship that exists between what a student already knows and how the student is to learn new information and skills.

CBA supports instruction by controlling the amount, frequency, and difficulty level of material presented to each individual learner. We learn as individuals, even when we exist in a group. It is necessary to build on our *prior knowledge*, an idea that, at the time, was also being promoted by the increasingly popular learning concepts of Piaget and Vygotsky (Blake & Pope, 2008). For example, Piaget's learning theory incorporated the term *disequilibrium* to describe the state that exists when new information cannot be assimilated into existing knowledge. Prior knowledge serves as a basis on which to build new knowledge, which is most effectively provided in small increments (chunks) added to prior knowledge at a ratio that Betts (1946) called the *instructional level* (see also Hargis, 2013). This is a principal aspect of CBA, and one that is featured in the CBA-ID approach presented in this book.

Historically, CBA emerged at a time when a plethora of instructionally relevant learning theories were emerging after the overwhelming influence that B. F. Skinner and behaviorism had had on the study of learning and instruction. Preceding the development of CBA by more than a decade, and based conceptually in the operant conditioning framework, was the development of another instructionally focused form of assessment. At the University of Kansas, Ogden Lindsley (1992), with his colleagues, was pioneering a form of assessment that they called precision teaching.

> Precision Teaching boils down to "basing educational decisions on changes in continuous self-monitored performance frequencies displayed on 'standard celeration charts'" (Lindsley, 1992, p. 51). As such, it does not prescribe what should be taught or even how to teach it: "Precision teaching is not so much a method of instruction as it is a precise and systematic method of evaluating instructional tactics and curricula" (West & Young, 1992, p. 114). (Athabaska University, 1997–2013)

At about the same time that Gickling's CBA was emerging, Stanley Deno and his associates at the University of Minnesota were producing yet another form of assessment, which also drew data directly from the student's response to instruction. It seemed appropriate to include a full description of Deno's (1985) model in the special issue of *Exceptional Children*, which Deno provided in his article "Curriculum-Based Measurement: The Emerging Alternative." Deno added the term *curriculum-based measurement* (CBM), which had first appeared the previous year (Fuchs, Deno, & Mirkin, 1984). The resulting exponential growth in the popularity of the CBM model is now well known. The primary difference between CBM and CBA is that CBM takes less time and is easily norm-referenced, while CBA remains focused on the instructional match between the individual learner's prior knowledge and the instructional level of that learner.

Shortly after the 1985 special issue on CBA, Alan and Emilie Coulter from Louisiana State University's College of Medicine began to provide training in CBA. Anticipating the need to more closely align CBA and direct instruction, the Coulters signified their approach under the name of *curriculum-based assessment for instructional design* (CBAID; Coulter & Coulter, 1989). The positive influence of their extensive training in Louisiana and Pennsylvania has had a lasting effect that is still felt in those states and elsewhere, but the Coulters never formally published their materials.

It is reasonable to assume that the rise of CBA and CBM in the 1980s and 1990s led to the development of the subsequently popular categorization of authentic assessment, which had been introduced by Grant Wiggins in 1989 and "conveys the idea that assessments should engage students in applying knowledge and skills in the same way they are used in the 'real world' outside of school. Authentic assessment also reflects good instructional practice, so that teaching to the test is desirable" (Marzano, McTighe, & Pickering, 1993, p. 13). Teaching to the test today refers to teachers spending valuable instructional time preparing students to take the state accountability test, but when the assessment process represents the real world, then teaching to the test is simply preparing students to apply what they learn in meaningful ways.

Authentic assessment has served as a general category for what has also been called alternative assessment. Why all the different assessment terms? The whole purpose of assessment became confounded when it became the primary vehicle for determining eligibility for federally funded special programs. We educators, in our attempt to recapture the value of basic instructional assessment, were determined to find the language that would bring us back to that basic purpose of assessment—to improve the academic achievement of individual students.

In the fifth edition of their textbook on assessment, Salvia and Ysseldyke (1991) partially resolved the situation with a description of CBA. In addressing various forms of informal assessment, they stated that

> over the past decade there has been a significant increase in curriculum-based assessment. Curriculum-based assessment includes (1) direct observation and analysis of the learning environment, (2) analysis of the processes used by students in approaching tasks, (3) examination of pupil products, and (4) control and arrangement of tasks for students. Focus is on assessment of a student's ongoing performance in the existing curriculum. (pp. 26–27)

Later editions of this text did not include this description, undoubtedly because the world of assessment had become much more varied both in available options and available approaches.

In *A Practical Guide to Alternative Assessment*, Herman, Aschbacher, and Winters (1992) described the situation this way:

> Dissatisfaction with existing standardized testing coupled with unabated faith in the value of systematic assessment have given rise to proposals for new assessment alternatives. Whether we call these alternatives performance testing, authentic assessment, portfolio assessment, process testing, exhibits, or demonstrations, the hope is that they will better capture significant and enduring educational outcomes. While proposed assessment strategies may be diverse, they share a common vision. (p. 6)

A few pages later, they add that

> these new assessments stress the importance of examining the processes as well as the products of learning. They encourage us to move beyond the "one right answer" mentality and to challenge students to explore the possibilities inherent in open-ended, complex problems, and to draw their own inferences. (p. 9)

The following year, Marzano and colleagues (1993) tersely stated that "the term alternative assessment applies to any and all assessments that differ from the multiple-choice, timed, one-shot approaches that characterize most standardized and many classroom assessments" (p. 13).

And, so, the list began to grow. Today, it includes such traditional terms as *formative and summative assessments*, *formal and informal assessments*, *qualitative and quantitative assessments*, and *diagnostic assessment*. But the list also contains so-called new terms in assessment: *common assessments, universal screeners, progress monitoring*, and *performance assessment* (Landrigan & Mulligan, 2013).

In order to reiterate just what CBA was intended to be in the beginning, I quote Ed Gickling: "Curriculum-based Assessment is a procedure for determining the instructional needs of a student based upon the student's ongoing performance within existing course content" (Tucker, 1985, p. 200). There are three vital points in that definition. First, CBA is a procedure for determining the instructional needs of a student. Assessment data, even if they are drawn from the student's performance in his or her curriculum, that do not translate directly into instructional strategies to improve that student's performance, do not constitute CBA as described in this book. It may be that CBM is very useful in making decisions about the student's program or placement, but unless the data provide a direct link to instructional strategies, the process is not CBA.

The second vital point in this definition is that it is drawn from the student's ongoing performance. Assessment of ongoing performance implies a frequent measurement of student behavior, certainly not just a quarterly or annual review.

Finally, all CBA data are drawn from the student's performance within existing course content, which means from within the curriculum of the general (regular) educational program of the school that the student attends. Obtaining performance data from an alternate curriculum or from some standardized item pool of controlled instructional objectives is not CBA.

The reading consultant and the school psychologist use CBA, as thus described, to help the teacher determine how the student is performing in the required coursework of the school, whether or not that performance is at the "instructional" level, what the instructional level is (if the student is not at that level already), and whether or not performance improves with appropriate instructional intervention.

In the end, it does not matter whether you call the process CBA, CBM, consultation, old-fashioned teaching, high-tech "instructionetics," or direct instruction and feedback. What matters is that you frequently obtain data from the student's performance in his or her required course of study and use those data to guide his or her instruction in order to improve performance. And that is just what Matthew Burns and David Parker have provided in this book. In *Curriculum-Based Assessment for Instructional Design*, Burns and Parker describe a number of "authentic" (research-based) strategies and tools for assessing the student's prior knowledge, existing skill level, and preferred mode of learning in order to maximize the instructional process. Indeed, in this book, Burns and Parker have developed a natural and practical extension of a conceptual format that was originally called, simply, curriculum-based assessment. The book provides much-needed clarification of the several terms that have been used over the past three decades, and it provides hands-on application of the instructional principles involved.

JAMES A. TUCKER, PhD
University of Tennessee at Chattanooga

REFERENCES

Athabasca University. (1997–2013). *Precision teaching: Concept definition and guiding principles.* Retrieved from *http://psych.athabascau.ca/html/387/OpenModules/Lindsley/introa1.shtml.*

Audette, R., & Coulter, W. A. (1981). Interview-based assessment. In J. A. Tucker (Ed.), *Non-test-based assessment* (pp. U1–U2, S1–S10, T1–T37, W1–W49, R1–R7). Minneapolis: National School Psychology Inservice Network, University of Minnesota.

Betts, E. A. (1946). *Foundations of reading instruction.* New York: American Book Company.

Blake, B., & Pope, T. (2008). Developmental psychology: Incorporating Piaget's and Vygotsky's theories in classrooms. *Journal of Cross-Disciplinary Perspectives in Education, 1*(1), 59–67.

Coulter, W. A., & Coulter, E. M. (1989). *Curriculum-based assessment for instructional design (CBAID): The trainers handbook.* New Orleans, LA: Directions and Resources Group.

Deno, S. L. (1985). Curriculum-based measurement: The emerging alternative. *Exceptional Children, 52,* 219–232.

Durkin, D. (1984). Is there a match between what elementary teachers do and what basal reader manuals recommend? *The Reading Teacher, 37,* 734–745.

Ellis, A. K. (2005). *Research on educational innovations* (4th ed.). Larchmont, NY: Eye On Education.

Fuchs, L., Deno, S. L., & Mirkin, P. K. (1984). The effects of frequent curriculum-based measurement and evaluation on pedagogy, student achievement, and student awareness of learning. *American Educational Research Journal, 21*(2), 449–460.

Gickling, E. E., & Armstrong, D. L. (1978). Levels of instructional difficulty as related to on-task behavior, task completion, and comprehension. *Journal of Learning Disabilities, 11,* 559–566.

Gickling, E. E., & Havertape, J. F. (1981). Curriculum-based assessment. In J. A. Tucker (Ed.), *Non-test-based assessment* (pp. U1–U2, S1–S23, T1–T93, W1–W59, R1–R36). Minneapolis: National School Psychology Inservice Network, University of Minnesota.

Hargis, C. H. (2013). *Curriculum-based assessment: A primer.* Springfield, IL: Charles C. Thomas.

Hall, R. V., & Hall, M. (1981). Observation-based assessment. In J. A. Tucker (Ed.), *Non-test-based assessment* (pp. U1–U2, S1–S17, T1–T16, W1–W17, R1–R2). Minneapolis: National School Psychology Inservice Network, University of Minnesota.

Jenkins, J. R., & Pany, D. (1978). Standardized achievement tests: How useful for special education? *Exceptional Children, 44,* 448–453.

Landrigan, C., & Mulligan, T. (2013). *Assessment in perspective: Focusing on the reader behind the numbers.* Portland, ME: Stenhouse.

Lindsley, O. R. (1992). Precision teaching: Discoveries and effects. *Journal of Applied Behavior Analysis, 25,* 51–57.

Marzano, R. J., McTighe, J., & Pickering, D. (1993). *Assessing student outcomes: Performance assessment using the dimensions of learning model.* Alexandria, VA: Association for Supervision and Curriculum Development.

Mercer, J., & Ysseldyke, J. E. (1977). Designing diagnostic intervention programs. In T. Oakland (Ed.), *Psychological and educational assessment of minority children* (pp. 70–90). New York: Brunner/Mazel.

Salvia, J., & Yesseldyke, J. E. (1991). *Assessment* (5th ed.). Boston: Houghton Mifflin.

Samuels, S. J. (1984). Basic academic skills. In J. E. Ysseldyke (Ed.) *School psychology: The state of the art* (pp. 17–35). Minneapolis: National School Psychology Inservice Training Network, University of Minnesota.

Tucker, J. A. (Ed.). (1981). *Non-test-based assessment: A training module.* Minneapolis: National School Psychology Inservice Training Network, University of Minnesota.

Tucker, J. A. (1985). Curriculum-based assessment: An introduction. *Exceptional Children, 52,* 199–204.

West, R. P., & Young, K. R. (1992). Precision teaching. In R. P. West & L. A. Hamerlynck (Eds.), *Designs for excellence in education: The legacy of B. F. Skinner* (pp. 113–146). Longmont, CO: Sopris West.

Wiggins, G. (1989). Teaching to the (authentic) test. *Educational Leadership, 47*(7), 41–47.

Acknowledgments

We gratefully acknowledge Natalie Graham, Editor at The Guilford Press, for her guidance and Dr. Chris Riley-Tillman for his support.

Matthew thanks Dr. James Tucker for getting him started on this path over 20 years ago and for teaching him everything he knows about CBA-ID, assessment, consultation, and leadership.

David thanks Kristen McMaster and Stephanie Al Otaiba for engaging him in early writing research that led to initial extensions of CBA-ID to writing, where the concepts and ideas hold great promise.

We also gratefully acknowledge the pioneering work of Ed Gickling, Alan Coulter, Joe Kovaleski, Sylvia Rosenfield, Ed Shapiro, and Jim Ysseldyke, who have all shaped our research and careers in ways and to an extent that they probably do not even realize.

Finally, we both thank our beautiful wives and families for continuous support and inspiration, and Matthew in particular thanks his children, Matthew and Kathleen, for being frequent "test subjects" and for starring in several CBA-ID training videos.

Contents

Purchasers of this book can download
and print additional copies of the Appendices
from *www.guilford.com/burns2-forms*.

CHAPTER 1

Curriculum-Based Assessment for Instructional Design
Using Data to Drive Instruction and Intervention

Most of you reading this book have been or will be challenged by a student with whom you work. Take a moment and recall or predict your course of action. If it was a reading problem that you were confronting, then you probably sat down with the student and listened to him or her read. If it was math, then you probably gave the student some problems to solve and examined his or her work carefully. A writing problem required you to sample the student's writing and to dive deeply into the content and form with which it was written. Our guess is that probably none of you went to the student's cumulative file to pull his or her state accountability test score. In fact, there probably was not a single score anywhere in his or her history that was particularly useful.

Kame'enui and Simmons (1990) provide an outstanding instructional framework in which they differentiate observable from nonobservable academic behavior. Math and writing are observable because they result in a product that

> **The first step in determining student needs is to make reading observable, sample the behavior, and interpret what you see.**

can be examined. There are cognitive processes involved that cannot be seen, but they can be deduced based on the written product. Reading is completely nonobservable. Thus, the first step in determining student needs is to make reading observable, sample the behavior, and interpret what you see. That is why teachers and interventionists place such a high value on hearing the child read for themselves.

We are both former practicing school psychologists who conducted hundreds of academic assessments as part of learning disability identification evaluations. Some schools in which we worked had reading or math specialists who generously offered to conduct the academic assessments for us to lighten our respective loads, but each time we gratefully and respectfully declined. We felt responsible to help the team develop goals, objectives, and plans for the students and could not get a clear picture of the children's strengths and needs without directly observing their performance in the academic task. We were not watching the students' performance while completing standardized norm-referenced tests of reading, math, or writing, but we still produced data that were extremely useful to instruction.

CURRICULUM-BASED ASSESSMENT FOR INSTRUCTIONAL DESIGN

One piece of information that teachers and interventionists try to obtain directly from observing performance is a student's instructional level, or the appropriate balance between task expectations and student performance that results in the best learning. Teachers all strive to teach students at their own "instructional level." In fact, the term *instructional level* is probably one of the most used, and most important, in all of education. There are multiple opinions about how to best determine a student's instructional level, and some that vary quite a bit from one another. They range from very informal (e.g., having a student put a finger down each time he or she comes across a word that he or she cannot read, and if he or she puts five fingers down for any one page, then the book is too difficult) to using an expensive and time-consuming published reading inventory. Many of the data approaches used to measure an instructional level are problematic and will be discussed in detail in Chapter 3. We advocate for an approach called curriculum-based assessment for instructional design (CBA-ID), which is the single most powerful instructional tool that we have ever encountered. CBA-ID is the subject of this book.

In 1977, Ed Gickling coined the phrase *curriculum-based assessment* (Coulter & Coulter, 1990) to refer to systematic assessment of the "instructional needs of a student based upon the ongoing performance within the existing course content in order to deliver instruction as effectively as possible" (Gickling, Shane, & Croskery, 1989, pp. 344–345). There are several aspects of this definition that are highly desirable. It makes explicit the goal of delivering instruction as effectively as possible. Ongoing performance refers to frequent monitoring of student progress, and frequently assessing student growth is a critical aspect of effective instruction (Fuchs & Deno, 1991) and of any intervention model (Shapiro, 2011). Using the course content implies a more authentic assessment, which is clearly and intuitively desirable to most teachers, and efficiency is important in today's resource-limited schools.

The administration procedures and psychometric properties will be extensively discussed throughout the text. However, CBA-ID for reading essentially requires having the student read for 1 minute from classroom reading material (e.g., basal reader, chapter book, content-area book) while recording the number of words read correctly, which is then divided by the total number of words in the sample to create a percentage of words read correctly. The percentage is then compared to an instructional level criterion of 93–97%.

Math and writing procedures also involve sampling the behavior and comparing the data to an instructional level criterion, but that will be explained in subsequent chapters.

Research has consistently demonstrated that using CBA-ID data to determine a student's instructional level led to increased reading fluency (Burns, 2002, 2007; Roberts & Shapiro, 1996; Shapiro, 1992; Shapiro & Ager, 1992), math skills (Burns, 2002), and student time on task (Gickling & Armstrong, 1978; Treptow, Burns, & McComas, 2007). There has also been considerable research regarding the reliability of CBA-ID data (Burns, Tucker, Frame, Foley, & Hauser, 2000; Burns, VanDerHeyden, & Jiban, 2006; Parker, McMaster, & Burns, 2011) and the validity of resulting decisions (Burns, 2007; Burns & Mosack, 2005), which is discussed in further detail in Chapter 3.

The Use of CBA-ID in Practice

Although CBA-ID results in psychometrically sound data (Chapter 3) and has consistently improved student learning, fewer than one-third of practitioners surveyed used CBA-ID (Shapiro, Angello, & Eckert, 2004). The utility of CBA-ID for instruction is that the data are used to determine a student's skill level relative to the material and then modify the instruction to provide an appropriate level of challenge. As stated earlier, teachers and interventionists clearly understand the importance of providing an appropriate challenge, and research has consistently identified the effectiveness of doing so, but CBA-ID remains mysteriously an infrequently applied yet powerful instructional tool.

There are two potential reasons why CBA-ID is underutilized in schools despite convincing research evidence. First, there are not clearly articulated procedures in the literature. The only comprehensive texts discussing procedures used within CBA-ID are unpublished manuals by Gickling and Havertape (1981) and Coulter and Coulter (1990). Later, Enggren and Kovaleski (1996) produced a manual regarding CBA-ID through the Pennsylvania Instructional Support Team. Beyond those manuscripts, there are only infrequent book chapters and some web-based information, but no published book(s). Compare the lack of published administration procedures with the sources available regarding curriculum-based measurement (CBM; Deno, 1985), and it becomes clear that more has been written on how to use curricular assessments to measure progress (CBM) rather than systematically target instruction (CBA-ID). Both CBA-ID and CBM were created during the same time period to be alternatives to standardized achievement tests. However, CBM was discussed in at least three separate books published by major publishers (Hosp, Hosp, & Howell, 2006; Shinn, 1989, 1998) and administration procedures are readily available on several websites. Thus, there is an obvious need for clearly articulated administration procedures for CBA-ID in a widely available source.

A second reason why CBA-ID is underutilized could be conceptual confusion. Despite the appealing components of the definition for CBA espoused by Gickling and colleagues in 1989, it has also created some difficulties. The term CBA referenced a specific model of assessment that was first articulated by Gickling and Havertape in 1981, but it has subsequently come to refer to essentially any model that uses the curriculum to collect data about individual students. Thus, Coulter and Coulter (1990) coined the term CBA-ID, which in our opinion is an elegant and accurate term for a powerful model, and it is the term that we use throughout this book.

CBA-ID and Instructional Assessment

Although the term CBA-ID differentiated the assessment model from other approaches, there remained some conceptual confusion with other models that shared the "curriculum-based" name (e.g., curriculum-based measurement and curriculum-based evaluation), despite multiple articles that compared and contrasted CBA-ID and CBM (Burns, MacQuarrie, & Campbell, 1999; Rosenfield & Shinn, 1989). Thus, as the assessment model evolved, the name did too and Gickling and colleagues subsequently starting using the term *instructional assessment* (IA) due largely to confusion over several assessment models that all use the term *curriculum based* (Gravois & Gickling, 2008).

Although IA is a powerful instructional tool, there are some potential difficulties with using the term in reference to the assessment model first described by Gickling and Havertape (1981). First, Kame'enui and Simmons (1990) used the term IA to refer to a model in which academic difficulties were defined according to "instructional influences on a learner's opportunity to succeed" (p. 22) such as task demands, response requirements, types of assessments used, and assistance provided during assessments. The conceptual framework for the Kame'enui and Simmons IA model was Mosenthal's (1982) pyramid, in which the success on any given task is interdependent with the instructional setting, materials, teacher, and student. It involves selecting a task, identifying the objectives within a task, assessing the objectives, analyzing student response, and designing an intervention plan.

> **Success on any given task is interdependent with the instructional setting, materials, teacher, and student.**

Gravois and Gickling's (2008) model is similar to Kame'enui and Simmons's (1990) in that both involve targeting specific material, sampling student behavior with the material, and identifying skills that need additional support. However, Gravois and Gickling's model is more fluid and dynamic, and organically moves and changes throughout the assessment. Thus, the latter model allows for more flexibility, but it is difficult to standardize. Gravois and Gickling (2008) state that "the student's listening capacity and concept familiarity with the curriculum being taught in the classroom are assessed by reading to the student and then speaking with the student about what was read" (p. 9), but nowhere do they discuss how to do so or how to judge student responses. They go on to state that within IA the assessor is "observing the student's prior content knowledge, listening capacity, and oral language capacity to comprehend and respond to grade-level material," but do not provide guidance on how to do so, and implementation guidelines for math and writing are not explicitly discussed.

Gravois and Gickling conduct trainings regarding IA through ICAT Resources (*http://icatresources.com/index.cfm*), and we both speak highly of their skills as trainers. However, a review of research regarding Gravois and Gickling's (2008) model concluded that there is sufficient research to support it, but it cannot be implemented unless the model architects train you directly (Burns, 2004c). One of the basic aspects of an effective innovation is that it can be implemented correctly on a large scale, and that it is still effective once it is taken from the guru who developed it (Ellis, 2005). Moreover, IA is an assessment technique for which the reliability and validity should be confirmed, and data cannot be reliable if they are obtained from an unstandardized assessment model.

CBA-ID as we conceptualize it is different from both IA models. The original manual (Gickling & Havertape, 1981) and the IA manual from Pennsylvania (Enggren & Kovaleski, 1996) both focus heavily on assessing the instructional level, but the Gravois and Gickling (2008) chapter regarding IA only discusses the instructional level as a principle of quality instruction and does not outline how to assess it. Thus, focus of the assessment evolved from 1981 to 2008 and IA became a more comprehensive assessment-to-intervention system.

Coulter and Coulter (1990) suggested that the CBA model that eventually became IA needed to be more standardized so that it could be easily taught to future and current practitioners, and easily researched. All of the published research regarding the psychometric properties and the effectiveness of the assessment model first articulated by Gickling and Havertape (1981) was conducted in regard to assessing the instructional level (e.g., Burns, 2007; Burns et al., 2000; Gickling et al., 1989). We also believe that assessing the instructional level is an important aspect of the assessment process with direct implications for intervention and instruction. Therefore, we agree with Coulter and Coulter and differentiate CBA-ID from IA in that CBA-ID is only one aspect of the overall IA model, but it is at the very core of the approach.

Figure 1.1 provides a pictorial depiction of the IA model and where CBA-ID fits into it. We merged both the Gickling and Havertape (1981) IA model with the Kame'enui and Simmons (1990) model into one comprehensive description.

The assessment process starts by selecting which academic area to target. Reading assessments can be driven by the National Reading Panel (2000) in that practitioners can collect data regarding phonemic awareness, phonics, fluency, vocabulary, and comprehension to determine the appropriate intervention target. Math can be guided by a curriculum's scope and sequence. Writing can be targeted by collecting data on student writing samples relative to curricular expectations. After determining which intervention target, the assessor decides which objectives to assess and gathers or creates assessment materials to represent the objective. Knowledge about the student's background knowledge and skills should help determine what to assess.

Once the objectives and assessment materials are determined, practitioners can use CBA-ID procedures to sample performance. Using CBA-ID to conduct the performance assessment outlined by both models allows for practitioners to use a well-researched and standardized approach for this important aspect of the assessment model. Moreover, the instructional level provides an empirically derived and well-researched criterion that was developed specifically to design instruction and intervention, which provides a more defensible criterion for comparing data (Kame'enui & Simmons, 1990).

> **The instructional level provides an empirically derived and well-researched criterion that was developed specifically to design instruction and intervention.**

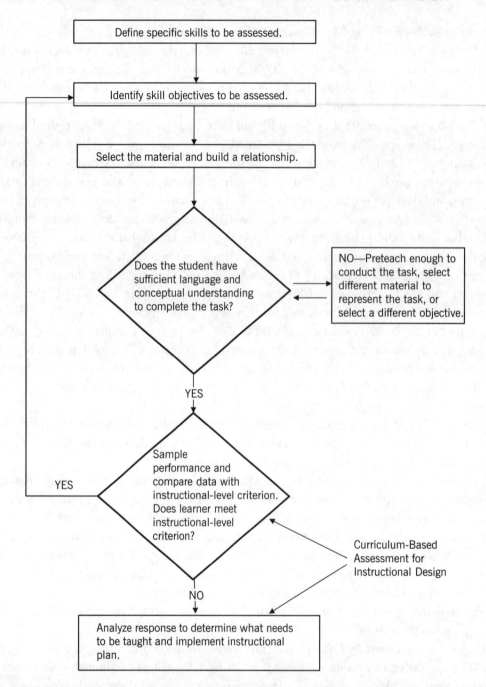

FIGURE 1.1. IA model based on Gravois and Gickling (2008) and Kame'enui and Simmons (1990) that incorporates CBA-ID.

CBA-ID and Response to Intervention

There has been a recent resurgence of interest in assessment-to-intervention models such as CBA-ID, IA, and curriculum-based evaluation because schools are implementing response to intervention (RTI) with increasing frequency. RTI is the practice of providing quality instruction and intervention, and using student learning in response to that instruction to make instructional and important educational decisions (Batsche et al., 2005). Most schools are easily implementing some aspects of RTI such as universal screening and monitoring progress. However, in our experience, schools are struggling to develop and implement Tier 2 (small-group supplemental) and Tier 3 (individualized) interventions.

CBA-ID provides data that are especially useful for addressing the instructional planning components of RTI (Burns, Dean, & Klar, 2004), and assessing how closely a student skill level matches the difficulty of a given task is one of the functional variables for student learning associated with RTI (Gresham, 2002). Therefore, teachers and interventionists could use CBA-ID to conduct a survey-level assessment to determine the appropriate Tier 2 intervention. Once a lack of consistency between instructional material and student skill is identified with CBA-ID, then task difficulty can be modified to meet the needs of the individual student (Daly, Witt, Martens, & Dool, 1997; Dickinson & Butt, 1989; Treptow et al., 2007). Alternatively, interventionists can preteach curricular material to create an instructional level before the learning activity occurs for students with intense learning needs (Beck, Burns, & Lau, 2009; Burns, 2007).

THE BOOK

As discussed above, CBA-ID was first introduced in an unpublished document, but that was printed before nearly any research regarding CBA-ID was conducted. The exception was Gickling and Armstrong's (1978) initial study that demonstrated the importance of the instructional level (discussed in Chapter 2). A few occasional book chapters (e.g., Gickling & Rosenfield, 1995; Gravois & Gickling, 2002, 2008) discuss CBA-ID, but none provide administration procedures. Other books (Jones, 2008; Salvia, 1989) also include the words *curriculum-based assessment* in their titles, but use the term more generally and do not refer to CBA-ID. The result of the lack of published administration procedures, along with several published but inferior assessments of the instructional level, results in the instructional level being one of the most misused and misunderstood concepts in education today.

The current book is the result of 20 years of experience and research, and was motivated by our frustration regarding the lack of use of this powerful instructional tool. In fact, we argue that there is no one singular tool that is more powerful for designing intervention or aligning instruction to student needs, but we have found that most classroom teachers seem to be unaware of this easy technique. Educators can use this book to add a quick and easy tool to their repertoire. After working as school psychologists, we both left our positions as practitioners to become consultants and educational researchers. CBA-ID has become the cornerstone of our consultation efforts and research agendas. We have used it with children who are learning disabled in reading (Burns, 2007; Burns, Dean, & Foley, 2004) and math (Burns, 2002), children with behavioral difficulties (Beck et al., 2009), English language learners (Burns & Helman, 2009), and young children (Bunn, Burns, Hoffman, & Newman, 2005).

The goal of this book is to translate our experience and research into easy-to-use administration procedures. CBA-ID is almost as easy as listening and counting. Of course, it takes some level of expertise to translate the data into practice, but after reading this book you will be able to improve the education of the students who you serve the very next day. It also only requires a few minutes to complete a CBA-ID; compare that with the lengthy standardized tests that do not result in instructionally relevant data and do not have the strong research base associated with CBA-ID. The next time you are confronted with a challenging student, you will be armed with a powerful technique and will confidently embark on a process that will make a difference. Chapter 2 of the book provides perhaps the most comprehensive description of the instructional level ever published and how it fits within instruction and intervention, and Chapter 3 discusses CBA-ID as an assessment tool and compares it with other assessment approaches such as informal reading inventories. Chapters 4 through 6 describe administration procedures for contextual reading, reading skills, math procedures, math concepts, and writing. Chapter 7 outlines the use of CBA-ID for teachers, special education teachers, and interventionists. Finally, Chapter 8 presents several examples of how to use CBA-ID in groups and with individual students.

CHAPTER 2

The Instructional Level

Why do students fail? There are many reasons why a student might not successfully perform an academic task including they are not motivated, they need more help with it, or it is too hard (Daly et al., 1997). The last potential reason is directly addressed by considering the student's instructional level. The first is addressed indirectly because one of the reasons students may not want to do a task is that it's too easy. Academic and related behavioral difficulties are typically viewed from a CBA-ID perspective to be the result of a mismatch between student background knowledge and skill and the curriculum. The curriculum can be too difficult, which results in student frustration and subsequent behavioral and academic difficulties, or it can be too easy, which results in student boredom. CBA-ID attempts to find "the window of learning" (Tucker, 1985, p. 201) between boredom and frustration, which we call the instructional level.

Essentially our jobs are to collaborate with teachers and school professionals who work with the most challenging students. We typically start the consultation/research process by talking to the teacher about his or her concerns for individual students. Whenever the concern involves frequent off-task behavior, our first step is to assess whether the student can read. In our experience, most of the behavioral problems in the schools are at least linked to academic deficits.

We once worked with a second-grade student who was diagnosed as emotionally impaired (referred to as *emotional–behavioral disorder* in federal special education law) and who exhibited severe behavior problems. One day I (M. K. B.) was paged by the school that Tom (pseudonym) attended and he raced over to find Tom in the principal's office lying on the floor. The principal was attempting to hold Tom, who was only in second grade and relatively small for his age, in a restraining hold that he had learned in a recent training, the special education teacher was trying to restrain his wildly kicking legs, and the school social worker was kneeling next to Tom pleading, "Tell us what you are thinking." It was a disturbing scene. However, the social worker then asked Tom to draw out what he was thinking and Tom agreed. Reluctantly, the principal and special education teacher released him and he went to a nearby table to draw his thoughts. Tom's resulting picture was an incredibly clear demonstration of the link between academic deficits and behavioral difficulties because he drew a stick-figure picture of a child at a desk with his head down and with thought bubbles across the top. In the thought bubbles he had written "I can't do it," "It's too hard," and "I'm dumb!"

Further analysis with Tom indicated that most of his behavioral outbursts occurred during reading and math instruction. Thus, our intervention plan for Tom certainly included social skill training and so on, but also included academic interventions designed to reduce the mismatch between what we were expecting and what Tom was capable of doing. Just to be clear, we are not saying that Tom was incapable of the work; we are saying that the required tasks were not appropriate for Tom because he did not have the necessary background knowledge and skills. Imagine how you would behave if you were asked to read a statistics book for 30 minutes.

There are students who experience behavioral difficulties for reasons other than frustration with academic tasks, but unfortunately, Tom's story is not an uncommon one. There are many reasons why students can display academic and behavioral difficulties, but frustration is often the cause. Roberts, Marshall, Nelson, and Albers (2001) used CBA-ID procedures to identify an instructional level as part of a functional behavioral analysis with students who exhibited high off-task behavior. Reducing student frustration by ensuring an appropriate instructional level leads to decreased off-task behavior. Two reasons why students become frustrated during academic tasks are because they are completing a task that is too difficult, or they are required to learn too much information. We discuss both below.

> **Two reasons why students become frustrated: (1) they are completing a task that is too difficult, or (2) they are required to learn too much information.**

FRUSTRATION BECAUSE THE TASK IS TOO DIFFICULT

Reading for Comprehension

The first reason that students become frustrated is that the task is just too difficult. Imagine if we agreed to give you $5 million to play professional basketball and all you had to do was be good enough to score about 12 points each game against the best basketball players in the world. The $5 million reinforcer would be highly motivating, but if you are not athletic, or if you are under 6 feet tall, then probably all of the motivation in the world is not going to get you to world-class status as a basketball player. Imagine how frustrating that would be. Sometimes asking a student to read a book that he or she cannot read is the equivalent of asking you to guard LeBron James, and all of the points, tokens, grades, and other reinforcers are not going to change that. The encouraging point here is that, although not all students can be coached into a professional-level sport, we strongly believe educators can make instructional decisions that help all students develop successful academic skills.

Gickling (1984) categorized academic tasks into one of two categories: reading for comprehension (i.e., getting meaning from print) or drill (i.e., all other tasks, such as writing, spelling, and subskills of reading such as word attack and sight-word recognition). He also theorized that students should be able to read 93–97% of the words to create an instructional level for reading and 70–85% of the items for drill tasks (Gickling & Thompson, 1985). Although the term *drill* has a somewhat negative connotation in education, we will continue to use Gickling's dichotomy to address certain domains of learning. However, we have found that there are other domains, such as math and writing, in which the instructional level needs to be conceptualized differently.

Take a moment and try to read the passage below, which contains 123 words. A total of 30 words (25%) were randomly selected to be scrambled, and the order of letters within those 30 words was randomly determined. Thus, 75% of the words are not scrambled.

Meat-Eating Plant

Vahe you ever dahre of a aemt-gantei plant? The Venus **flytrap** is one nikd of aemt-eating plant. The tyrfpla has meat-gantei leaves tiwh sihra on ehtm. It grows to be about one foot tall.

Teh Venus flytrap eats escisnt. The insides of its seealv are filled with sweet, sticky juice. An insect touches the hairs on the leaves when it siter to get to the tesew eijcu. Hist tells teh seealv to shut. The hairs on the leaves move together and colk in the insect. Now the insect is paptdre. The tncsie dies and is food for the tyrfpla. When the tyrfla gets yurnhg naaig, it seonp its seealv to htcca another insect. After eating many insects, the leaves die.

Some of you probably felt challenged by the task of reading the passage above and wanted to conquer it. Some probably thought it was boring and silly, but for some of you, the task seemed too difficult to really attempt and you probably gave up while trying to read the second line. The data presented in Figure 2.1 are based on Gickling and Armstrong's (1978) study that first demonstrated that students will give up or become bored. The students represented in the figure were five second-grade students who were first observed during reading instruction. The students were all diagnosed with a learning disability in reading. As can be seen in the figure, the students completed about 65% of the tasks, were on task about 50% of the time, and comprehended about 20% of what they read prior to the authors making any changes to the instructional material. The authors then used material in which the students could read 85% of the words, and there was little change. However, the researchers then used instructional material in which the students could read 93–97% of the words correctly. Task comprehension and completion went up, which makes some intuitive sense, but time on task also went up to over 90%! The researchers then did something brilliant: They used material in which the students could read 100% of the words and task completion and comprehension remained high, but time on task went down to the original levels. In the first phase that they made a change, the students could read less than 93% of

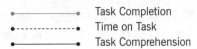

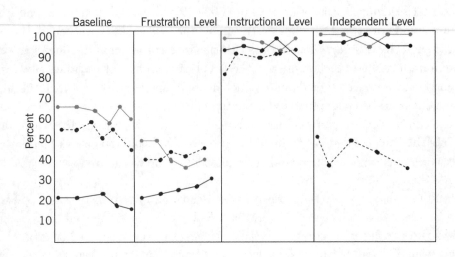

FIGURE 2.1. Time on task, task comprehension, and task completion for second-grade students. Based on Gickling and Armstrong (1978).

the words and experienced frustration. In the final phase, the students could read 100% of the words and experienced a mastery level and were bored.

One would expect a linear relationship between student skill and performance: The more a student knows, the better he or she will do. However, the relationship is actually

> **When it comes to student learning, easier material is not always better.**

curved, as in Figure 2.2, in which student background knowledge and skill is too high for the assigned task and student performance goes down presumably because of boredom. Think of that gifted and talented student who acts up out of boredom. Umbreit, Lane, and Dejud (2004) analyzed the off-task behavior of a fourth-grade student and found that he was not

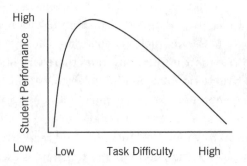

FIGURE 2.2. Simple relationship between task difficulty and student performance.

being sufficiently challenged. When they provided more challenging material, the student's time on task increased from about 50% to about 90% in both math and reading. We also frequently see teachers provide easier material to support struggling students, but they then provide material that is too easy, which results in boredom and poor performance. The teachers may then interpret the poor performance as a lack of skill and then provide material that is even easier still. When it comes to student learning, easier is not always better. Thus, we have to provide an appropriate level of challenge that is not too difficult, but not too easy either.

At this point we should clarify what we mean by student performance. Material that is too easy can, of course, produce accurate responding, as depicted by the final phase of Figure 2.1. The students had very high comprehension and task completion, both indicators of good academic performance. However, we consider student performance also to include task engagement. A number of reasons can be offered for why task engagement is an important indicator of academic performance, from research finding a strong relationship between on-task observations and learning (Gettinger & Seibert, 2002) to the common observation that students who are not appropriately challenged stop trying and often fall behind. Figure 2.2 shows overall academic performance, and low task difficulty corresponds with low overall academic performance because of the importance of task engagement.

Drill Tasks

Research has consistently supported that providing a student reading material in which he or she can read 93–97% of the words increases several outcomes, such as time on task, task completion, and task comprehension (Burns, 2002; Gickling & Armstrong, 1978; Treptow, Burns, & McComas, 2007). However, 93–97% is for tasks that involve skill performance, such as reading for comprehension, and there are several other types of tasks. Drill tasks (e.g., sight words, math facts, spelling words, letter sounds) involve learning specific quantities of new information, and are another type of task that can be too difficult for students.

A ratio of known items to unknown was hypothesized to achieve an instructional level for drill tasks (Gickling & Thompson, 1985). Different ratios have been suggested, including 70–85% known and 15–30% unknown (Gickling & Thompson, 1985), 30% unknown to 70% known (Coulter & Coulter, 1990), 50% unknown to 50% known (Neef, Iwata, & Page, 1980), and more challenging ratios of less than 50% known (Robinson & Skinner, 2002). Tucker (1989) presented a model called incremental rehearsal (IR), which could be applied to many different drill ratios, but Tucker's example used 10% unknown to 90% known.

Roberts, Turco, and Shapiro (1991) found that 50% unknown or 40% unknown to 60% known resulted in more sight words being acquired during drill sessions, as compared with less challenging ratios (70–85% known), but less challenging ratios (20% unknown to 80% known) led to better retention. We directly compared different ratios and found that students retained substantially more items and were on task more frequently when they were taught with 90% known items as compared with more challenging ratios (0% known, 50% known, or 83% known; Burns & Dean, 2005b).

The data presented in Figure 2.3 are based on Burns and Dean (2005b) and show the effect that ratios of known words had on retention of learned items and of time on task. The data were collected from five fourth-grade students (three boys and two girls) who were identified with a learning disability in reading and significant attention difficulties. We taught them 10 common words from a sight-word list, observed their time on task during the intervention sessions, and tested their retention 1 week later. As you can see from the figure, the students were most on task when they participated in the session with 90% known and remembered the greatest number of words from that condition. Thus, we recommend that practitioners use a high ratio of known items, one that approximates 85–90% known, when practicing new items such as sight words, math facts, letter sounds, spelling words, and so on.

Providing a high ratio of known to unknown items in practice is not difficult. Skinner and colleagues (Cates & Skinner, 2000; McCurdy, Skinner, Grantham, Watson, & Hindman, 2001; Skinner, Fletcher, Wildmon, & Belfiore, 1996) interspersed easy math items within more difficult items (e.g., include a single-digit multiplication problem every third problem within a multidigit multiplication practice sheet) and found that students actually preferred the tasks that interspersed the easier items even though it meant that they had to complete more items. Additional examples include providing review spelling words when students practice spelling units, or incorporating review letters when teaching new letter sounds.

Tucker's (1989) IR model is a direct application of the instructional level to drill tasks. IR is a flash-card drill method that intermixes unknown items with items already known at a ratio of one unknown to nine known. The unknown items are then rehearsed in the following manner:

First unknown, First known

First unknown, First known, Second known

First unknown, First known, Second known, Third known

First unknown, First known, Second known, Third known, Fourth known

First unknown, First known, Second known, Third known, Fourth known, Fifth known

First unknown, First known, Second known, Third known, Fourth known, Fifth known, Sixth known

First unknown, First known, Second known, Third known, Fourth known, Fifth known, Sixth known, Seventh known

First unknown, First known, Second known, Third known, Fourth known, Fifth known, Sixth known, Seventh known, Eighth known

First unknown, First known, Second known, Third known, Fourth known, Fifth known, Sixth known, Seventh known, Eighth known, Ninth known

> Teaching words with a high proportion of known items can mitigate the effects of student-level variables.

We discuss IR further in Chapter 7, but previous research has consistently demonstrated it to be an effective intervention with large effects (Burns, Zaslofsky, Kanive, & Parker, 2012).

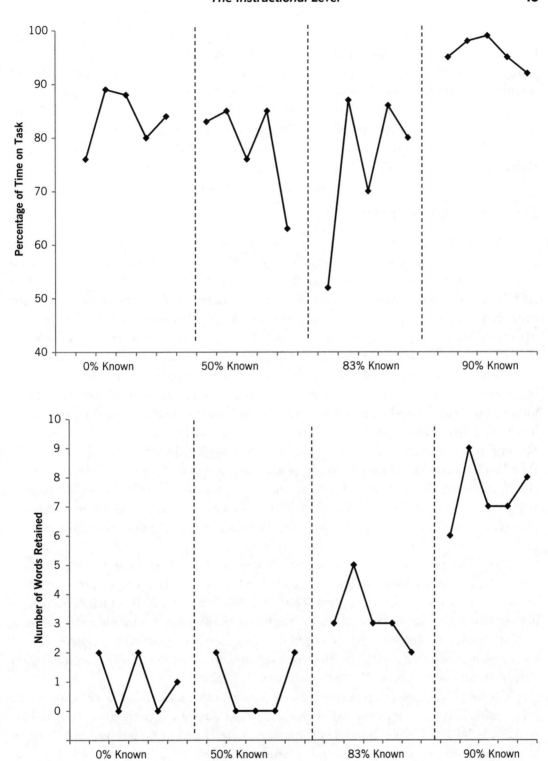

FIGURE 2.3. Student time on task and retention with four levels of known material within a drill task.

A previous study taught sight words to first-grade students and found that interspersing known words with IR resulted in 91% retention, but the students only retained 76% of the words taught with all unknown items (Nist & Joseph, 2008). Moreover, how much a student retains is directly related to student-level variables, such as verbal intelligence, but teaching words with a high proportion of known items can mitigate the effects of student-level variables. The correlation between verbal intelligence and number of sight words retained fell to –.07 when the words were taught with 90% known items (MacQuarrie, Tucker, Burns, & Hartman, 2002).

Expectancy and Interest

Many learning theories discuss the role of the expectancy–value theory of motivation (Eccles et al., 1983). Essentially, expectancy–value theory states that student performance will be determined by the student's expectation for success and the degree to which the student sees the task as important or interesting. Expectancy–value theory is a powerful concept for instruction. However, many educational professionals focus too much on the value part and not enough on the expectancy aspect. It is not unusual for teachers to provide a student a choice in selecting reading material as an intervention to increase the likelihood that he or she will actually read the book. Although we fully support doing so, that is only one aspect of the task that teachers should consider. Below we provide an example of how we used an intervention that focused on providing high-interest reading material, but also compared it with a different intervention that used the instructional level to increase time on task. Students who are interested in a topic will be more engaged when reading about that topic. Based on the value side of the expectancy–value theory, it makes sense that selecting material about which the student expresses an interest would enhance the motivation to read the text, and a relationship does seem to exist between interest and reading comprehension (Bray & Barron, 2003–2004; Schiefele, 1999). However, we wanted to learn more about the expectancy side of the expectancy–value theory.

The relationship between student engagement in academic tasks and achievement is well documented (Gettinger & Seibert, 2002). Engagement is the student's active involvement in the learning task (Reeve, Jang, Carrell, Jeon, & Barch, 2004), which is frequently assessed through behavioral measures such as time on task or words read correctly per minute (Appleton, Christenson, Kim, & Reschly, 2006). Moreover, poor task completion is the most frequent behavioral concern for which children are referred to school psychologists (Bramlett, Murphy, Johnson, Wallingsford, & Hall, 2002).

Although the relationship between interest and comprehension has been studied, the relationship between interest and student engagement was only hypothesized (Bray & Barron, 2003–2004; Schiefele, 1999). Thus, it makes sense that time on task would be related to interest, but research has consistently linked task difficulty with time on task (Burns & Dean, 2005b; Gickling & Armstrong, 1978; Treptow et al., 2007). The example that follows demonstrates how we examined the relationships among interest (value), material difficulty (expectancy), and task engagement.

Students and Materials

The three students were Amy, a Hispanic American female, Denise, an African American female, and Wayne (all pseudonyms), a Caucasian male. Each student was nominated by his or her teacher as having low on-task behavior. After identifying potential participants, a screening procedure was conducted to confirm teacher reports. The screening consisted of having each student silently read a grade-level passage (ranging between 150 and 200 words) that was randomly selected from the Read Naturally (RN) reading series (Read Naturally, 2003; described below), and occurred while all students in the class completed a similar activity. The participating students were observed using a momentary time-sampling procedure with 10-second intervals. Each session ranged from 5 to 10 minutes in length, with a total of three screening sessions. The mean percentage of time on task for participating students while reading the passage was 80.97%, with a standard deviation of 19.73% and a range from 64.2% to 100%.

We used RN passages to test our question, which is a reading program consisting of a collection of 24 stories for each of 13 sequenced levels of reading difficulty ranging from first through eighth grade. We used passages that ranged in length from 110 (grade 2) to 465 (grade 8) words.

Amy also read passages selected from the Qualitative Reading Inventory–4 (QRI-4; Leslie & Caldwell, 2006). This was because her frustration level extended beyond the levels included in the RN program. The QRI-4 provides text at levels from preprimer to high school, and is designed to provide information about when a student can and cannot identify words and answer comprehension questions correctly. For Amy, stories representing high school difficulty were selected for frustration-level passages; the length of each was approximately 600 words.

Task Difficulty

After screening for time on task, reading skills were screened with CBA-ID using passages taken from the RN program. The examiner recorded known and unknown words while each participant read aloud from a passage for 1 minute. Words were recorded as known if read correctly within 2 seconds, and unknown if they were read incorrectly, omitted, or the student hesitated for more than 2 seconds. Participants then read passages that were progressively harder or easier until the percentage of words read correctly fell within the 93–97% correct range. Frustration-level passages were created by using passages from the grade level that fell two levels above the instructional level (e.g., if instructional level equaled 4.0, then frustration level would be 6.0). The frustration-level passages were then confirmed by measuring the percentage of words known within the passage, which fell below 92% known.

Amy's instructional level from the RN passages was found with the grade 8.0 material, with 94.6% words read correctly. This placed her frustration level at the grade 10.0 material. An instructional level was found for Denise with the grade 2.0 material, with 95.5% words read correctly, which placed her frustration level at grade 4.0. Finally, Wayne's instructional level for reading was at grade level 5.0, with 97.4% words read correctly, which placed his frustration level at 7.0.

Topical Interest Level

The instructional or frustration level represented two levels of the independent variable designed to test the effects of the expectancy side of the expectancy–value theory, and topical interest (Renninger, 2000) was the independent variable used to test the value side. Once each participant's instructional and frustration levels were found within the RN passages, the students were then shown all 24 passages from both corresponding levels. The participants viewed the title, the passage, and a single illustration for each passage and were asked to rate their interest in the passage on a scale from 1 (not at all interesting) to 5 (very interesting). The results of this interest survey were then grouped into low interest (1's and 2's) and high interest (4's and 5's) for both instructional- and frustration-level passages to create four conditions: high-interest instructional level, high-interest frustration level, low-interest instructional level, and low-interest frustration level.

Time on Task

A momentary time-sampling procedure similar to the screening procedure was used to record intervals of time that participants were observed exhibiting on-task behavior. At each 10-second interval, the observer scanned the participants and recorded whether on- or off-task behavior occurred. On-task behavior was defined as attending to the reading material (e.g., looking at the reading material; Shapiro, 2004). Off-task behaviors included leaving the seat, looking at any point other than the paper, talking to peers, reading something other than the assigned passage, purposeless movement of the passages, and focusing attention on peers (Shapiro, 2004). The length of time to read the passage was not limited, but required less than 10 minutes for each session. Students were instructed to complete individual quiet activities when finished with the reading task, at which time the observation for each participant stopped.

A multielement single-subject design was used in which one of the four experimental conditions was administered in randomized order for each participant during each session. The conditions were changed after each session, resulting in rapid alternating administrations of the four experimental conditions, which is consistent with multielement designs. A total of 21 sessions were conducted, with Amy and Wayne each participating in all sessions, and Denise participating in 17. Two sessions were conducted each day with at least 30 minutes between sessions, and data were collected 4 days per week for 2 weeks and 2 days during a third week. The final data point was collected during the only session on the last day of the study. The sessions took place during the whole-class setting, in which all 25 students were given a passage from RN and were instructed to read it silently. No assistance was given during sessions except to clarify instructions.

Data collection began by distributing a copy of the RN passage to the entire class. Participating students received an individualized RN passage representing one of the four conditions for that student. Nonparticipating students received a grade-level passage. All students where then told to read their stories silently and when they were done they were asked to take out a quiet activity until the entire class was finished. Observation ended for each participating student when he or she turned the passage over after completing the task; no observational data were collected while students worked on the quiet activity.

Results

As can be seen in Figure 2.4, the frustration level with low-interest condition (FL-LI) consistently resulted in fewer intervals on task than the other conditions, but there was little differentiation among the three conditions. The mean percentage of on-task intervals for the FL-LI condition for Amy was 89.1% (*SD* = 6.79%), 89.12% (*SD* = 10.92%) for Denise, and 76.32% (*SD* = 12.60%) for Wayne. All other conditions were above 90% for all three students except frustration level with high interest (FL-HI) for Wayne, which resulted in 74.84% (*SD* = 13.48%) intervals that were on task. With the exception of the FL-LI and FL-HI conditions for Wayne, each condition represented a general increase in on-task behavior over baseline; but little differentiation was observed in the graphed data, suggesting that no interaction effects were found.

In order to compare more directly the effectiveness of each independent variable, data were combined into the two levels for each variable. In other words, data were considered at the instructional level without regard for the interest level and interest level was considered without regard for difficulty. Figure 2.5 compares passages read at the instructional and frustration levels and Figure 2.6 compares high- and low-interest passages. There was clear differentiation between the two conditions in Figure 2.5 with the instructional-level passages resulting in higher on-task behavior. The average percentage of intervals rated as on task for Amy was 97.3% (*SD* = 2.85%) for the instructional level and 89.8% (*SD* = 5.7%) for frustration, Denise's data resulted in a mean percentage of on-task intervals of 98.3% (*SD* = 4.7%) for instructional level and 90.0% (*SD* = 9.2%) for frustration, and Wayne's mean on-task behavior was 94.6% (*SD* = 10.8%) for instructional level and 75.6% (*SD* = 12.4%) for frustration. For each participant, the increase over baseline was greatest during instructional-level conditions.

The data presented in Figure 2.6 directly compare high- and low-interest conditions without regard for task difficulty and do not result in clear differentiation. The average percentage of on-task intervals for Amy was 94.7% (*SD* = 3.5%) for high-interest passages and 94.8% (*SD* = 7.2%) for low-interest passages, Denise's data resulted in a mean on-task percentage of 93.9% (*SD* = 7.4%) for high interest and 94.0% (*SD* = 9.6%) for low interest, and Wayne's mean percentage of on-task behavior was 86.2% (*SD* = 15.4%) for the high-interest condition and 83.3% (*SD* = 15.1%) for the low-interest condition.

Level of task difficulty affected time on task, but the rated level of topical interest did not. A direct interpretation of the data suggests that task difficulty contributed more to on-task behavior than interest. That is not to say that there is no value in providing students choices based on interest because doing so may increase the reinforcing value of completing the task. However, practitioners should be sure to consider instructional modifications on

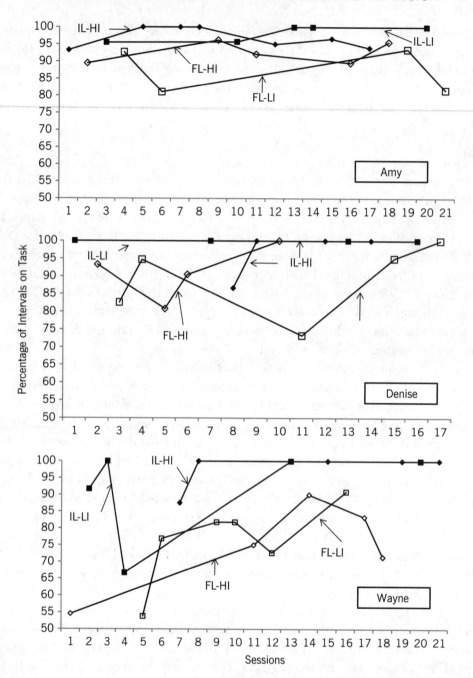

FIGURE 2.4. Student time on task during the four reading conditions. FL, frustration level; IL, instructional level; LI, low in interest; HI, high in interest.

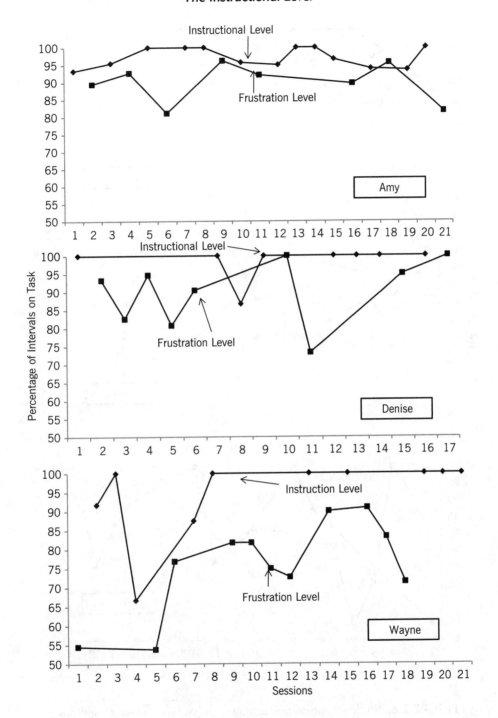

FIGURE 2.5. Student time on task during instructional- and frustration-level conditions.

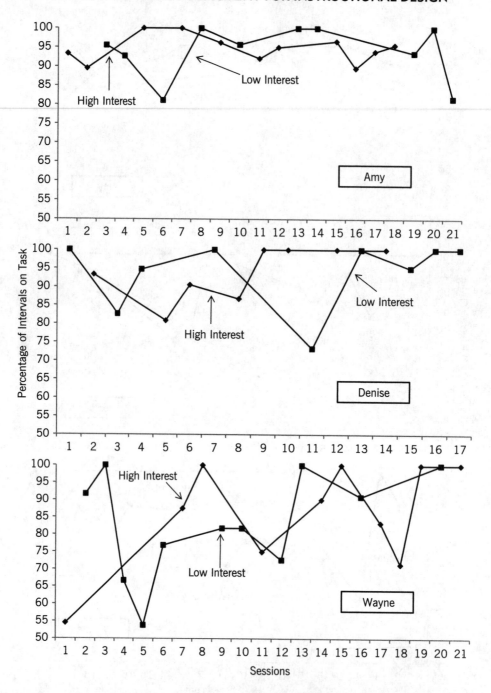

FIGURE 2.6. Student time on task during high- and low-interest conditions.

task difficulty a priority for designing interventions for low task completion or time on task. Using reading material with 93–97% known words will likely increase student time on task, but the effects of other stimulus-related variables remain unknown. Our interpretation of these results is that having elementary-age students read material that is of high interest to them is probably fine, but it will not be effective if they cannot read the words. The results regarding task difficulty demonstrate that when students do not know a high percentage of words, their performance will likely be poor. Unfortunately, we have not replicated this investigation with high school–age students.

FRUSTRATION FROM BEING TAUGHT TOO MUCH

A second reason why students become frustrated is that we are presenting too much information at one time. Research has consistently demonstrated that working memory increases as children get older, and there are many reasons why students' memory capacity can vary, including prior experience with the information (Rabinowitz, Ornstein, Folds-Bennett, & Schneider, 1994), content of the material (Scweickert & Boruff, 1986; Semb & Ellis, 1994), and developmental factors (Fry & Hale, 1996; Gathercole & Baddeley, 1993; Miller & Vernon, 1996).

The optimal size of an instructional set of material is called the acquisition rate (AR; Gickling & Thompson, 1985), which is defined as the amount of information that a student can successfully rehearse and later recall (Burns, 2001). Take a moment and recall a recent all-day workshop; the kind that is often used in school-based professional development. Now that you are thinking of one, take another moment to try and recall specific things that you learned during that day-long learning session. Can you think of any? Now, remember how you felt at the end of the day. You probably felt physically exhausted even though you sat in a chair all day. Finally, imagine that you are a 15-year-old, 10-year-old, or 6-year-old. Would you have sat still feeling like that, or would you have walked out?

> The optimal size of an instructional set of material is called the *acquisition rate*, or the amount of information that a student can successfully rehearse and later recall.

Examine the data presented in Figure 2.7. The data are based on previous research with fourth-grade students identified with attention-deficit/hyperactivity disorder but who were not medicated (Burns & Dean, 2005a). We taught each student 10 words. Each data point is the average number of off-task behaviors for the students as we taught that word number. For example, in the top half of the figure, the two students averaged 0.25 off-task behaviors per minute as they learned the first word (i.e., one off-task behavior every 4 minutes) and 0.35 off-task behaviors per minute while learning the second word.

As you can see from the figures, two of the students had an AR of 2 and three had an AR of 4. The frequency of off-task behaviors increased for the students as the session progressed, but there was a dramatic jump as we attempted to teach the word that exceeded

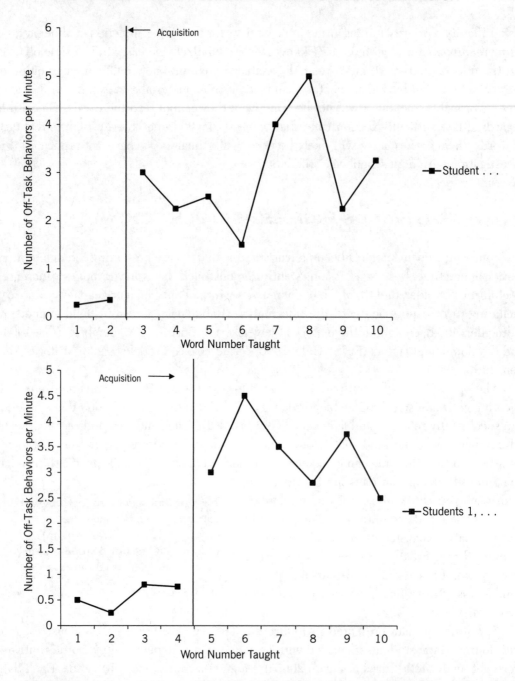

FIGURE 2.7. Percentage of time off-task before and after exceeding students' AR.

the AR. Both groups went from less than one off-task behavior per minute to an average of one off-task behavior every 20 seconds.

The concept of an AR is consistent with cognitive interference. In 1967, Ceraso found that attempting to teach too much information at one time reduced the retention of previously learned material. For example, consider a common scenario where a teacher attempts to teach 10 spelling words in one lesson. If a student can retain only five items (i.e., the AR), then attempting to teach the remaining six through 10 items will not only lead to poor retention of the five latter items but will also reduce the retention of the first five and would likely increase student frustration and resulting off-task behavior while teaching them. This phenomenon was called retroactive cognitive interference and occurred when learning a new item reduced recall of a previously learned item.

The concept of retroactive cognitive interference led to the somewhat common practice of using shortened or distributed learning sets versus massed practice, which has consistently been shown to lead to better recall (Cepeda, Pashler, Vul, Wixted, & Rohrer, 2006; Donovan & Radosevich, 1999). Currently, there is convincing evidence that students recall a higher percentage of learned items when they are taught, for example, in sets of five rather than 10. However, when providing intervention to individual students, it would also be ineffective to teach only two or three items if the student can recall five, just as it would be ineffective to teach five items when the student can only recall three. We discuss AR more thoroughly in Chapter 3 and include procedures to assess it.

Multidimensional Instructional Level

As stated in Chapter 1, the term *instructional level* is bantered around in education with incredible frequency partially because teachers intuitively understand the importance of providing an appropriate level of challenge. However, most approaches to contextualizing the instructional level are too simplistic and the resulting measurement of it is psychometrically unsound (e.g., informal reading inventories). The relationship between student performance and task difficulty is not linear, as indicated in Figure 2.2. Tasks can be too easy or too difficult, with too-difficult tasks resulting in frustration and too-easy tasks resulting in boredom, and both scenarios reduce overall academic performance. However, simply considering task difficulty does not capture the entire picture.

> **Interventions can include the right amount of task difficulty, but because the wrong amount of material is used, learning outcomes are still unacceptably low.**

We contextualize the relationship between student performance and task demands as multidimensional, as indicated in Figure 2.8. Teachers should consider two factors when attempting to match an instructional level: the difficulty of the material and the amount of new information being presented. The figure depicts graphically the challenge that teachers encounter daily with struggling students; interventions can include the right amount of task difficulty, but because the wrong amount of material is used, learning outcomes are still unacceptably low. Conversely, the right amount of material could be used, but because it is too difficult, learning remains low.

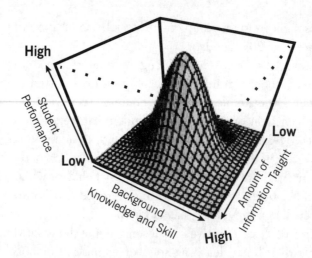

FIGURE 2.8. Three-dimensional instructional-level model.

We contextualized task difficulty in Figure 2.8 as level of background knowledge and skill to move away from grade-level expectations. Many practitioners might assume that a particular grade level represents a student's instructional level. For example, it is easy to assume that the instructional level for a student is third grade and provide material written at a third-grade level for that student. However, that thinking is problematic for two reasons. First, not all books supposedly written at "third-grade level" present an equal challenge. Second, most approaches to providing grade-level estimates for instructional level are seriously flawed (e.g., informal reading inventories), in that the passages written to represent a given level are not well constructed, do not represent the given grade level, and occasionally do not even match the proposed difficulty hierarchy (e.g., third-grade passages are easier than second-grade passages).

More advanced approaches such as Lexile (MetaMetrics, 2013) are psychometrically preferable to informal reading inventories, but still cannot overcome the third difficulty with grade-level thinking for instructional level: it is almost impossible to generalize to the individual student. Research regarding Lexiles is conducted with large numbers of students, but in practice the data are used for individual children. How well a child interacts with a given set of reading materials has more to do with the background knowledge and vocabulary for the student than the supposed difficulty level with which it was written. We frequently see children who successfully read books with Lexile ratings beyond their recommended range because they have considerable background knowledge in the topic, and there is no way to measure that for individual students. Many teachers interpret the success and even enthusiasm for the supposedly too-challenging task as evidence for the importance of interest, but as discussed above, students will prefer tasks that they expect to complete. Thus, a student's excitement about reading a particular book will certainly be influenced by interest in the topic, but it is quite likely that the student's familiarity with the topic enhances his or her ability to actually read the words.

Exceeding student background knowledge and skill or teaching too much information can lead to frustration and behavioral difficulties. However, instructional efforts may not be optimal even if task difficulty is appropriate but too much or not enough information is presented. Figure 2.8 illustrates this by depicting low areas along the perimeters, where performance is inhibited due to a mismatch in task difficulty (back-left and front-right quadrants) or amount of material taught (back-right and front-left quadrants); when the appropriate amount of task difficulty is combined with the right amount of material, performance is maximized (center).

It is unusual to think of not presenting enough information, but student learning can be accelerated if, for example, we are able to teach four items rather than three each time we provide practice with math facts. Conversely, teaching an appropriate number of new items is one aspect of effective instruction, but students may not learn them sufficiently if contextualized within material that is too difficult (frustration) or too easy (boredom). Teachers and school psychologists need to find the "sweet spot" that represents the intersection of difficulty and quantity to enhance student learning.

Imagine if someone asked you to complete one simple task before you left school that day, just read a one-page document and prepare a very short summary for the staff meeting the next day. You might agree thinking that it is just one task, but then the person hands you the one-page document and it is written in Chinese. A small portion of you reading this book would mentally thank whoever taught them Chinese, but most of us would look at the person who made the request with anger, disappointment, and/or disbelief. Imagine the immediate frustration you would feel as you sat down to locate an online Chinese-to-English translator and painfully interpreted every single word. Consider the same scenario, but the person then hands you a 15-page document containing hundreds of two-digit multiplication problems to complete. Most of us could tackle a series of problems like 13×12 and 22×15 with little difficulty, but 15 pages of them?! Sure, you could complete the problems, but what is the point and how boring would that be? Unfortunately, children experience those two scenarios every day. Moreover, it is the student's perception of difficulty and value that matter rather than the reality of the situation. If you ask them to read a book and they do not see the value or do not expect to succeed, or if you ask them to complete math problems that they could do with some effort, but would require what they think to be an excessive length of time, then they will not take on these instructional tasks that most educational professionals would value.

THE INSTRUCTIONAL LEVEL AND THE LEARNING PROCESS

Although the instructional level is an important concept with direct implications for teaching and learning, it becomes an even more powerful tool when conceptualized within learning theory. We discussed expectancy–value theory above, but the learning hierarchy is also an important theoretical construct that has become a commonly used framework for intervention design (Ardoin & Daly, 2007). According to Haring and Eaton (1978), acquisition of new material is the first phase of the learning hierarchy and is characterized by slow and inaccurate performance in the skill. A student in the acquisition phase would require high modeling and immediate feedback. After a student becomes accurate, but still performs slowly, then he or she is operating in the fluency phase and would likely respond to repetition and overlearning procedures. Once the student can perform the skill with accuracy and sufficient speed, he or she then can generalize the newly learned information to different settings (Phase 3—generalization) and can apply it to different situations to solve problems (Phase 4—application).

As can be seen from the learning process described above, the accuracy with which the task is completed is potentially important information because two students with similar speed of responding may require different interventions based on their respective levels of accuracy. A student with low accuracy would need an intervention that targets accuracy, but a student with high accuracy would need an intervention that targets fluency. The instructional level could be the accuracy criterion that differentiates between the first two phases of learning. A student who is reading 95% of the words correctly, or who correctly completes 90% of a drill task correctly, would likely need a different intervention than a student completing a lower percentage accurately.

A recent example by Parker and Burns (in press) compared two commonly used reading interventions: repeated reading (Moyer, 1982; Rashotte & Torgeson, 1985; Samuels, 1979) and supported cloze (Rasinski, 2003). Most people are familiar with repeated reading, but supported cloze is an assisted intervention in which an instructor reads a passage jointly with a student. We asked the students to read every other word with an instructor in a given passage (e.g., instructor reads first word, student reads second word, instructor reads third word, student reads fourth word), and then to start over and switch the words read such that each word is both modeled for and read by the student. Repeated reading is a strong intervention that involves student practicing reading, but supported cloze specifically targets reading accuracy by modeling correct reading of words in the passage.

The two types of interventions map onto the learning hierarchy at different levels; supported cloze is an accuracy-focused intervention that targets the first stage of the learning hierarchy, whereas repeated reading is a fluency-focused intervention that targets the second stage. According to the learning hierarchy, fluency-focused interventions might not be as effective when a student is still in the accuracy stage of a learning task because he or she has not yet acquired the skills to accurately read words.

We were asked to work with three third-grade students with reading difficulties who were receiving 20 minutes of repeated reading every day, but who were not making progress. The first student was a Caucasian female named Julie, the second was a Caucasian male named Jim, and the third was a Caucasian male named Greg (all pseudonyms). All three scored below the 25th percentile on the *Measures of Academic Progress* (Northwest Evaluation Association, 2003), and scored below grade-level expectations on the fall benchmark assessment for oral reading fluency (i.e., 76 words read correctly per minute or less).

The students received repeated reading for 5 to 18 weeks before we started working with them. Unfortunately, none of the students read 93% of the words correctly during repeated reading, which suggested that this was not an appropriate intervention. We thought about continuing repeated reading with easier material, but decided to use supported cloze until they could read 93% of the words, at which time we switched back to repeated reading. It took Julie 10 weeks to consistently read 93% of the words correctly, Jim 9 weeks, and Greg 5 weeks.

Figure 2.9 displays oral reading fluency data for the interventions with the three students. The lines running through the data represent the slopes of the data and visually display the rate of growth. Examine the slopes while receiving repeated reading the first time. Julie's data were declining and although Jim and Greg were making some progress, it was not at a fast rate. These students were not reading accurately, thus they were slow and inaccurate, which represents the acquisition phase and suggests that an accuracy intervention was needed. Thus, we focused on increasing the accuracy of the intervention and once the students could accurately read at least 93% of the words, then their rate of growth increased dramatically. At that point, they were ready to receive a proficiency intervention that focused on increasing rate through practice (i.e., repeated reading). The slopes of the lines in the final phase for all three students were dramatically increased over the first phase despite both phases using the same intervention.

CONCLUSION

As Figure 2.8 shows, student performance is low when background knowledge is low and results in a difficult task, which is almost impossible to predict before beginning the task. The only way to determine whether the student has sufficient background knowledge is to have the student complete a sample of the task and assess percentage of known items with CBA-ID. We are not stating that teachers have to conduct a CBA-ID with every student in their classroom every time they want students to engage in independent or guided reading. We discuss the role of CBA-ID in general instruction more in Chapter 7. CBA-ID data are not as crucial for proficient readers who are growing as readers, as they are for struggling readers or for strong readers who have plateaued in their development. Providing an instructional level is always important, but there are more efficient ways to align instruction with student background knowledge for students who are not struggling. However, CBA-ID data are extremely useful to design instruction for struggling or difficult-to-teach students.

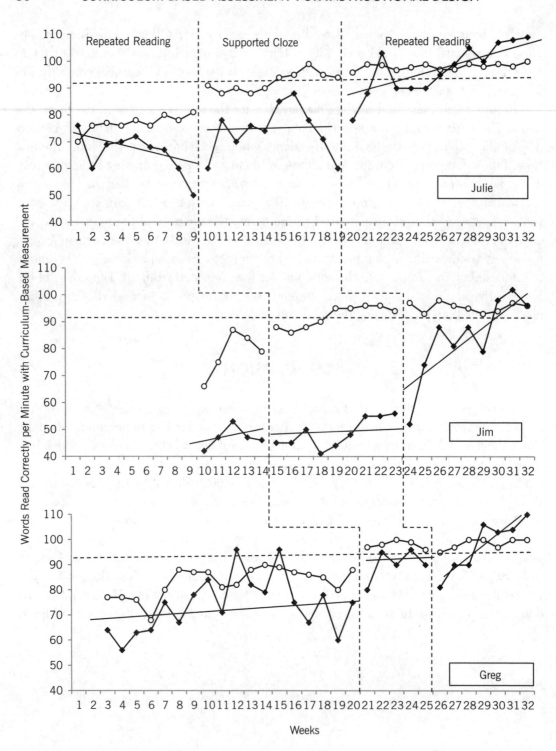

FIGURE 2.9. Oral reading fluency during repeated reading interventions before and after reading at instructional level.

CHAPTER 3

CBA-ID as an Assessment Tool

Effective teaching is, at least in one sense, the melding of assessment and instruction. There is a clear and strong link between assessment and teaching to the point that monitoring student learning is a core proposition for effective teaching by the National Board for Professional Teaching Standards (*www.nbpts.org/five-core-propositions*), and assessment is a basic standard for special education teachers (Council for Exceptional Children Board of Directors, 2004). When we were both practicing school psychologists we often taught students new information as a form of assessment to the point where onlookers inquired about the interventions we were conducting with students who were referred for a special education disability identification evaluation. Our response was "How can you determine if a child has a learning disability unless you watch the child during learning or without seeing if learning can occur?"

If assessment is so important to instruction, then why do teachers so often cringe at the sound of the word? It is because the educational community has lost sight of the power of assessment and has focused on the consequences of judgments made with the data. It may also be because of an unfortunate emphasis placed on summative approaches, which focus on producing data that summarize prior learning over formative approaches, which focus on producing data to inform future instruction (Stiggins, 2005). Determining if your students have met specific or global proficiency standards certainly plays a role in designing instruction because educators need to know whether our students learned the material to determine if we should reteach it. However, summative approaches provide minimal information for actually designing instruction. The accountability movement has changed teachers' and parents' perceptions of the word *assessment*.

When we talk about assessment, we are essentially talking about formative evaluation. The term *formative evaluation* is often misused to mean assessment that occurs before learning occurs, or monitoring student progress during learning (Linn & Gronlund, 2000; Salvia, Ysseldyke, & Bolt, 2007). In fact, curriculum-based measurement (CBM) has become synonymous with formative evaluation (Deno, 2003; Silberglitt & Hintze, 2005) because

CBM is so closely linked to monitoring progress. However, formative evaluation is best conceptualized as using data to identify student needs and to plan instruction that will better meet those needs (William, 2006). Formative evaluation is an ongoing feedback loop that simultaneously measures current student functioning and dictates future instructional activities. Progress monitoring is only one purpose for which data are used in the instructional process. CBM produces longitudinal data that are an excellent indicator of the rate of learning, but it seems to have somewhat limited utility in identifying specific strengths and difficulties for individual students (Fuchs, Fuchs, Hosp, & Hamlett, 2003). Certainly we should be monitoring student progress in the name of formative evaluation, but if that is all we are doing, than we are just barely tapping into the potential of a powerful instructional tool.

> **Formative evaluation is best conceptualized as using data to identify student needs and to plan instruction that will better meet those needs.**

CBA-ID AS A CORE COMPONENT OF FORMATIVE EVALUATION

Algozzine, Ysseldyke, and Elliott (1997) presented a model of effective instruction that included (1) planning instruction, (2) managing instruction, (3) delivering instruction, and (4) evaluating instruction. Formative evaluation should address all four phases, but much of the research attention has been on evaluating instruction. CBM seems ideally suited to evaluate the effectiveness of instruction and interventions, but CBA-ID seems better suited to plan, manage, and deliver instruction.

Planning Instruction

Setting goals is one of the basic tasks within planning instruction. Thus, educational professionals have developed several approaches to determining norm-referenced goals for CBM data. Normative goals are potentially useful for identifying students who need additional support (screening), but they provide little information to determine if a student has reached a level of proficiency. Does reading at the 50th percentile represent proficient reading? It may if the 50th percentile represents performance within the local norms of a high-achieving school or district, but in low-achieving schools or districts a student at the 50th percentile of the local norms may still be a very low reader. The point is that normative data alone do not adequately indicate successful skills.

A second component of planning instruction is deciding what to teach by "assessing skill levels to identify gaps between actual and expected level of performance" (Salvia et al., 2007). Although taking a fluency probe with CBM and comparing those data to local norms could accomplish this, this process does little to suggest *how* to close the gap between actual and expected performance. CBA-ID links data to intervention by suggesting the need for more or less challenging instructional material or by identifying specific items (such as unknown words in a reading curriculum), which can then be taught to the individual student. The instructional level of 93–97% known for reading is well researched

(Burns, 2007; Gickling & Armstrong, 1978; Shapiro, 1992; Shapiro & Ager, 1992; Treptow et al., 2007) and could serve as a potential criterion for planning what to teach. Students reading at a percentage of known material that fell below 93% could participate in efforts to increase the percentage of known words until the 93–97% known range is obtained, or students within the 93–97% range could participate in efforts to increase fluent reading. For example, a student in upper elementary could feasibly read 19 out of 20 words correctly (which is a low score for second grade and beyond) and still be within the instructional level (95%), but these data are much more useful than normative data alone. The normative data identify that the student is low in reading skills, but the CBA-ID data indicate that a proficiency-focused intervention is likely best because the student already reads accurately.

Finally, planning instruction involves pacing instruction appropriately. The longitudinal data of CBM are helpful for determining the student's pace of learning, but CBA-ID are more helpful for informing the teacher's pace of instruction. For example, ARs can be used to suggest the appropriate pace of instruction by determining how many unknown items can be taught before retroactive cognitive interference occurs. These data can be used to identify text levels that produce an appropriate number of unknown items so that learning can be maximized, but not frustrating.

Managing Instruction

Many of the tasks described as relevant to managing instruction involve various classroom management activities such as setting rules, teaching compliance, handling disruptions, and establishing a positive classroom environment. However, using time productively and maintaining academic focus were also emphasized. Teaching children at their instructional level increases task completion, task comprehension, and time on task (Gickling & Armstrong, 1978; Treptow et al., 2007), and exceeding a student's AR led to increased off-task behavior (Burns & Dean, 2005a). In fact, CBA-ID "is structured to help teachers plan instruction based on entry-level skills of students, thus maximizing on-task time during learning activities" (Gickling & Rosenfield, 1995, p. 588). There is certainly more to managing instruction and ensuring optimal academic learning time than using CBA-ID, but increasing time on task and decreasing behavioral difficulties are major components.

Delivering Instruction

Algozzine and colleagues (1997) also described showing enthusiasm, helping students value schoolwork, using rewards effectively, and modeling correct performance as part of the delivery of instruction. Activities more relevant to assessment practices, specifically CBA-ID, include assigning the appropriate amount of work, monitoring performance regularly, and providing opportunities for success while limiting opportunities for failure.

Standards for the assessment of reading and writing established by the International Reading Association (IRA) and the National Council of Teachers of English (NCTE; 1996) suggest that assessment data based on tasks that are either too easy or too difficult are not instructionally useful. Because CBA-ID assesses skills using tasks that match the individual student's skills, the data meet the IRA and NCTE standards and may be instructionally useful. In addition, most assessment models require some aspect of student failure (Hargis, 2005), but a basic goal of CBA-ID is obtaining high success rates for all students. Finally, teaching students at their individual instructional level increases student success and reduces the likelihood of student frustration (Gravios & Gickling, 2002). Thus, CBA-ID directly provides opportunities for success and seeks to limit student failure.

TYPE OF ASSESSMENT

CBA-ID can be useful to plan, manage, and deliver instruction, but has less utility to monitor progress. That is because CBA-ID measures specific skills rather than general outcomes. Within assessment, special education, and school psychology literature, there are generally two types of measures delineated: general outcome measures (GOMs) and subskill mastery measures (SMMs). A GOM is a standardized measure that assesses proficiency of global outcomes associated with an entire curriculum, and an SMM assesses smaller domains of learning based on predetermined criteria for mastery (Fuchs & Deno, 1991). The GOM and SMM data are each part of an integrated system of instructionally relevant data collection (Shapiro, 2011), and studies show positive outcomes when used together (Burns, 2002; Shapiro & Ager, 1992). We will discuss both below.

General Outcome Measures

GOMs are assessments of general outcomes and are often used to monitor progress, which involves frequently assessing children's academic development in order to make changes to instruction based on progress or a lack of progress (Speece, n.d.). The goal of GOM is to assess instructional effectiveness and quickly make changes as needed. Therefore, GOMs tend to be appropriate for and used as summative evaluations because the data are used to judge the effectiveness of instruction and may suggest a need for change. However, GOM data do not suggest what change is needed, only that one should occur. In fact, the Bloom, Hastings, and Madaus (1971) definition specifically lists "evaluation of progress" (p. 117) as an example of summative evaluation. GOM data can be critically important to the instructional process, but do not represent formative evaluation in and of themselves.

GOM data become more formative in nature when they are used to establish goals, which are important aspects of instructional planning (Algozzine et al., 1997), but summative evaluation samples learning tasks and formative evaluation examines all important aspects of the specific leaning unit (Bloom et al., 1971). Thus, formative evaluation probably cannot rely entirely on GOM data.

Subskill Mastery Measures

SMMs are more closely aligned with formative evaluation than GOM data because they are used to directly assess the learning unit to identify student strengths and needs before instruction occurs. For example, using CBA-ID to examine the percentage of words within an upcoming reading task can determine if the task will present an appropriate challenge, or if it will be too easy or too difficult. CBA-ID is an SMM because it focuses on specific skills such as reading a particular passage or book, completing a specific math objective (e.g., single-digit multiplication), or focuses on one particular aspect of writing. Moreover, data from CBA-ID are compared to a mastery criterion (i.e., the instructional or independent levels) rather than to a norm group. There are no percentile ranks for CBA-ID.

> **SMMs are closely aligned with formative evaluation.**

The focus in special education and school psychology research and practice has been on GOM because school psychologists were frequently involved in monitoring student progress. Moreover, the psychometric properties of GOM data tend to be stronger than SMM, or at least better established. However, as discussed below, there is considerable support for the reliability of CBA-ID data and the validity of the resulting decisions. Thus, teachers, school psychologists, and interventionists interested in conducting formative evaluation could consider CBA-ID an SMM that fits well into their assessment arsenal.

RELIABILITY AND VALIDITY OF CBA-ID

CBA-ID provides data that can be used to make formative evaluation decisions and teachers can use those data throughout the instructional process. However, standards regarding the use of educational assessments published by the American Educational Research Association, American Psychological Association, and the National Council on Measurement in Education (1999) state that the data derived from measures used in education should be reliable and should result in valid decisions. Teachers may not fully appreciate the importance of test reliability, but it is a concept with very real implications for classroom decisions. Every test has some level of error in it. Think back to a time in college or high school in which you did not prepare for a test quite like you should have. We are sure that even the most dedicated scholar occasionally did not adequately prepare for a PSYCH 100 exam or let that NAT SCI 201 exam sneak up on him or her. Now, of the times that you did not study as well as you should have, did you ever leave the exam session unsure how you did, but then received a pleasant surprise when the tests were handed back when you discovered that you actually did quite well? A more memorable alternative might be the time that you really prepared well for an exam, left the exam session confident that you aced the test, only to discover that the professor did not agree with your summation, which was reflected in a less-than-expected/desired grade.

In the two scenarios described above, did you feel that the test accurately represented your true knowledge? Every person has a true score that represents their true knowledge, skill, or aptitude. However, the observed score may not always exactly match a person's true score. The difference between the true score and the observed score is test error. Every test has some level of error. The question is how much error is acceptable? If you are using the test to determine whether you should reteach something, a relatively higher level of error would probably be fine because the consequence for getting it wrong would not be great.

However, if you used the data to decide if the child should be retained in the grade, be admitted into a graduate program, receive a monetary scholarship that could make college accessible, or be placed into special education, then the consequences for getting it wrong would be substantial and a much smaller amount of error would be acceptable. Reliability is an estimate of how free a test score is of error. In other words, a reliability of .90 suggests that 10% of the score is due to error. A reliability of .75 would have 25% error. Imagine telling parents that the score on a test suggests that their child has a reading disability when that score has 25–30% error!

> **Every test has some level of error. The question is how much error is acceptable?**

Data are considered reliable if they are consistent across time, forms, and scorers. Establishing the validity of decisions made with the data is a more complex process. The reliability and validity evidence for data derived from CBA-ID are discussed below.

Reliability

Reading

Burns and colleagues (2000) examined reliability estimates for assessing reading skills with CBA-ID using 93 general education students from second, third, and fourth grades. Results included interscorer reliability coefficients that ranged from .89 to .99, internal consistency coefficients of .87 to .96, alternate form-reliability estimates from .80 to .86, and test–retest coefficients that ranged from .82 to .96 for a 2-week test–retest interval. These data suggested that the percentage of known words within a reading task could be reliably measured across time, forms, and scorers. However, these data also examined reliability a second way in that the test–retest reliability estimates were computed by converting the data from a raw percentage to a category of frustration (less than 93%), instructional (93–97%), and independent (98–100%). The reliability of the category was then calculated by correlating the categorical score with a Tau coefficient, which resulted in coefficients above .80. Salvia, Ysseldyke, and Bolt (2010) suggested that coefficients of .80 or higher are needed for screening decisions about individual students and .90 or higher for important decisions (e.g., special education eligibility) about individual students. Thus, these data suggest that CBA-ID data from reading were sufficiently reliable for instructional decisions.

> **CBA-ID data from reading were sufficiently reliable for instructional decisions.**

Writing

The focus of the book to this point has been reading because most of the research around CBA-ID was in reading. However, there are CBA-ID procedures for writing and math as well. Early writing skills can be measured with different prompts depending on the student's skill. Picture–word prompts provide a word with a picture above it, and students write a sentence using the word provided. Sentence copying prompts provide simple sentences that students copy on lined paper. Both prompts require students to write for 3 minutes. Student responses are scored by counting the number of words written (WW), words spelled correctly (WSC), and correct word sequences (CWS). The assessment procedures are explained in detail in Chapter 6. Reliability estimates for these data all met or exceeded .70 across 2 weeks (Parker et al., 2011).

Math

CBA-ID for math is conducted by measuring specific skills within a curriculum. For example, a practitioner would assess a student using a timed probe of single-digit multiplication problems, but then would compute the number of digits correct per minute and compare that with an instructional-level criterion. Math assessment procedures are discussed in Chapter 5. Previous research among students in second through fifth grade found reliability coefficients of .64 for second and third grade and .85 for fourth and fifth grade (Burns et al., 2006). Five of the seven coefficients met or exceeded .70, and three exceeded .80. Moreover, the categorical data of frustration, instructional, or independent levels correlated across time with a coefficient of .42 for second and third graders, and .71 for fourth and fifth graders. Thus, data obtained from CBA-ID for math were sufficiently reliable for instructional decisions.

Acquisition Rate

The second dimension of CBA-ID, measuring ARs, was examined by Burns (2001) through estimates of delayed-alternate form reliability using sight-word recognition as the academic task. A total of 91 students from first, third, and fifth grades were taught unknown sight words until interference occurred, with the number of words learned and retained being recorded as the AR. The process was repeated 2 weeks later using different unknown sight words. Reliability estimates for ARs were .76 for first-grade students, .91 for third-grade students, and .91 for students in the fifth grade. The delayed-alternate form reliability coefficient for the total sample was .93. These coefficients suggested adequate reliability for instructional decision making.

Validity

Establishing the validity of decisions made with assessment data is more complicated than reliability. Content relevance is often considered a critical component of valid academic assessments (Messick, 1995), and is conceptualized as the extent to which the domain being measured is represented. One of the basic tenets of CBA-ID is that the assessment is ensured to match the curriculum because curricular content and objectives form the materials for the assessment. Unlike other curriculum-based

> **Unlike other curriculum-based approaches (e.g., CBM), CBA-ID does not utilize alternative curricula or standardized probes from a pool but instead uses the same curricular material for assessment and subsequent intervention.**

approaches (e.g., CBM), CBA-ID does not utilize alternative curricula or standardized probes from a pool but instead uses the same curricular material for assessment and subsequent intervention (Tucker, 1985).

Criterion-related validity is the extent to which data from one measure are related to data from an existing measure of the same or similar construct. Data obtained from math CBA-ID correlated with a standardized measure of math at .55, and the categorical data (frustration, instructional, or independent levels) correlated with the math measure at a coefficient of .14–.52 (Burns et al., 2006). Writing CBA-ID data correlated with a standardized measure of writing at coefficients that ranged from .26 to .52 (four out of six coefficients exceeded .40) for the raw data and .21–.50 (four out of six coefficients exceeded .40) for the categorical data (Parker et al., 2011). Finally, data obtained from measuring ARs with CBA-ID correlated with a standardized measure of memory at .70 with third- and fourth-grade students.

Construct validity is the extent to which a test or assessment procedure measures the theoretical trait or characteristic it purports to measure (Salvia et al., 2007). CBA-ID purports to measure the instructional level, which was defined by Gravois and Gickling (2002) as "a comfort zone created when the student has sufficient prior knowledge and skill to successfully interact with the task and still learn new information" (p. 888). Research has consistently demonstrated that using material that aligned to an instructional level for reading or math resulted in increased student learning (Burns, 2007; Treptow et al., 2007; VanDerHeyden & Burns, 2005b).

Research and theory regarding acqusition rates seems to be consistent with previous memory research. Several scholars have examined the limits of human learning (e.g., Fry & Hale, 1996; Gathercole & Baddeley, 1993; Miller, 1956). Brainerd and Reyna (1995) identified individual differences among students in their ability to acquire and retain new information, which suggest an individual capacity that might be affected by the content of the information (Scweickert & Boruff, 1986) or individual experience with the topic or data (Rabinowitz et al., 1994). Gregory (2000) argued that validity for assessment data could be suggested by evidence for consistency with expected developmental changes. ARs have been studied by cognitive researchers (Fry & Hale, 1996; Gathercole & Baddeley, 1993; Miller & Vernon, 1996), who have found a developmental effect on working memory with older children being capable of acquiring and retaining more information as compared with younger children. Burns (2004a) found a similar developmental trend for ARs of sight words, as measured with CBA-ID, but suggested that age no longer adequately predicted ARs after third grade. This latter finding was consistent with Gathercole and Baddeley (1993), who found that active rehearsal and consistent retention rates occurred between the ages of 6 and 8 years, which led to consistent individual differences in retention among students after the third grade. In other words, developmental effects accounted for variance among students until ages 6–8 years, afterward individual differences in rehearsal strategies were consistently used by students and accounted for differences in memory capabilities.

Of course, the ultimate test of how valid decisions are in education is how well using the data improve student learning (Kane, 2001). Modifying instruction based on CBA-ID data among students with a learning disability resulted in reading growth rates that exceeded students without disabilities for 66% of the students, and all students saw increases in their growth rates (Burns, 2007). Similar increases have also been noted for math (Burns, 2002; VanDerHeyden & Burns, 2005b), and exceeding a student's AR resulted in an immediate and dramatic increase in off-task behavior (Burns & Dean, 2005a). Therefore, CBA-ID results in data that are sufficiently reliable and have convincing evidence for validity.

CBA-ID COMPARED WITH OTHER ASSESSMENTS

The term *instructional level* is used frequently in education. In fact, there are multiple ways to assess a student's instructional level and there is a multi-million-dollar industry dedicated to doing so. However, many of those measures are problematic for reasons listed below.

Informal Reading Inventories

Betts coined the term *instructional level* in 1946, and unknowingly set in motion an entire industry. Many test publishers have created and sell various informal reading inventories (IRIs) including the Fountas and Pinnell Benchmark Assessment System (F&P; Fountas & Pinnell, 2007), the Basic Reading Inventory (BRI; Johns, 2005), Ekwall Shanker Reading Inventory (ESRI; Shanker & Ekwall, 2002), Qualitative Reading Inventory (QRI; Leslie & Caldwell, 2006), Burns and Roe Information Reading Inventory (B&R; Burns & Roe, 2007), and the Developmental Reading Assessment (DRA; Beavers, 2006).

IRIs vary somewhat in format, but almost all of them involve asking a student to orally read from grade passages while evaluating fluency, followed by answering comprehension questions. The student then reads progressively easier or more difficult passages until the teacher finds the highest level at which the student successfully reads the passage (as judged by acceptable fluency and answering a certain number of comprehension questions correctly). The highest passage at which the student reads successfully is identified as the student's instructional level.

IRIs have tremendous intuitive appeal and are commonly used in schools (Paris, 2002; Paris, Paris, & Carpenter, 2002). Despite widespread use, research on the appropriateness of using IRIs has been minimal at best. In fact, cautions against using IRIs have existed for 40 years (Walker, 1974). Below, we discuss psychometric and practical difficulties with using an IRI to assess students' reading skills.

> **Despite widespread use, research on the appropriateness of using IRIs has been minimal at best.**

Psychometric Difficulties

As described above, tests used for educational decisions should result in data that are sufficiently reliable for a given population and that promote valid decisions. CBA-ID has considerable research regarding reliability and validity, but rarely do publishers of IRIs report the reliability and validity estimates, and those that do often use questionable methods.

Spector (2005) reviewed tests manuals for common IRIs and found that most did not even report reliability. Assessment tools without reported reliability are the equivalent of a psychometric Ouija board; the information that they reveal might be accurate, but we have no way of knowing for sure. If an IRI reports that a student's instructional level is 3.0 grade level, the same test repeated the next day could result in 4.0, 2.4 the day after that, and perhaps as high as 4.6 the following day. Without acceptable reliability, we cannot have confidence in the data.

Many test publishers report correlations with IRI data with other reading measures as evidence for validity. However, correlations do not tell the entire story. Think of a set of scores in which Student 1 scored 98, Student 2 scored 95, Student 3 scored 91, Student 4 scored 88, and Student 5 scored 85. Next, to validate those scores, each student is given a second measure of the same skill and resulted in scores of 65, 63, 60, 55, and 50, respectively. Although the scores were different, the rank order stayed exactly the same, which would result in a very high correlation of .98. One could conclude this correlation as strong evidence for convergence, but what if the criterion for passing both tests was 70? Then, 100% of the students passed the first test, but 0% passed the second test.

We (Parker et al., in press) recently completed a study in which we examined the accuracy of decisions made with the F&P with over 800 students in second and third grade. We compared the F&P level score with a score from the Measures of Academic Progress for Reading (MAP-R; Northwest Evaluation Association, 2004), which is a nationally normed and well-constructed reading measure. The correlation between the F&P reading level and the MAP-R score was .76 for the second graders and .69 for the third graders. Again, these are high correlations, but the data resulted in a consistent decision with the MAP-R only 54% of the time. Therefore, if you wanted to use the data to identify students as needing additional support, you could spend thousands of dollars to purchase the materials, spend hours to train the teachers how to administer the test, dedicate hundreds of hours of instructional time to conducting the assessments, or you could invest 25 cents; simply take a quarter and flip it every time a student enters the door and you will get it right nearly as often.

Practical Difficulties

Besides psychometric considerations, what makes a good educational measure? Glover and Albers (2007) recommended that measures must be cost-effective, aligned with curricula, and time efficient. It would go beyond the scope of this book to review the costs for IRIs, but it suffices to say that IRIs require at least a moderate monetary investment for each assessment kit. Practical considerations are also closely related to time and use of the data. Most IRIs require approximately 20 to even 30 minutes to administer and are completed one-on-one. Thus, a classroom of 30 students would require anywhere from 600 (10 hours) to 900 (15 hours), which equates to 2 or 3 complete days to complete the assessment. Moreover, most schools use IRIs multiple times throughout the year, which could equal as much as 2 weeks of instructional time dedicated to completing the assessment. If the data were instructionally useful, then the time may be well spent, but the data would have to be critically important to warrant that much instructional time, not to mention human resource.

Measures must also be aligned with the curriculum being used. The overlap between major curricula and most IRIs is completely unknown. Moreover, the generalizability of the data is suspect. If a student scores an instructional level of 3.0, for example, the teacher still does not know what 3.0 means. How does that level correspond to other reading material? The F&P is part of a comprehensive system that includes books leveled to F&P levels. However, the publishers include no information about how those books were leveled or how well the score corresponds to the level of the books. We can tell you from experience that just because a student is measured to read at an M level and a book is supposedly written at an M, that does not mean that the student will be able to successfully read the book.

In addition to questions about correspondence between level score and reading level, we question the concept of reading level for individual students. As professionals who have worked with hundreds of students across the country, we frequently conduct various reading assessments with students. One time in particular the first author was leading a data collection effort that involved assessing oral reading fluency with several hundred elementary-age students. Thus, I (M. K. B.) spent an entire day listening to students read from graded passages taken from a highly respected measure of oral reading fluency. The task involved having each student read three separate probes and then recording the median score. Anyone who has conducted a large number of oral reading fluency assessments in 1 day can tell you, it can be a very boring task. I attempted to pass the time by recording the reading rate of students into a Microsoft Excel spreadsheet to see whether there were any differences in words read correctly per minute between boys and girls. Of the three passages, one dealt with dinosaurs and one dealt with cooking (I do not recall the topic of the third passage). At the end of the day, I was quite surprised to learn that the boys read the dinosaurs passage with statistically significantly higher fluency (as measured by words read correctly per minute) than the girls did, and the girls demonstrated significantly better fluency for the cooking passage than did the boys.

Although the finding described above might perpetuate gender stereotypes, it also made an important point. The three passages were supposedly written at the same grade level, but significant differences in readability occurred by gender group within the grade level. How well a child reads a particular passage has more to do with each child's individual background knowledge, vocabulary, and interest than it does the supposed difficulty level with which the book was written, and that information cannot be captured in any individual-level score, be it reported as a grade level (e.g., 3.0) or a readability level (e.g., level M). Data never generalize to or from the individual. If you administered an IRI to 100 students and matched the reading level to their score, you would probably have a decent match 50–66% of the time, but you would have no way of knowing for whom the match would not be aligned. Moreover, the more extreme the reading score, the less likely to match well. Thus, reading levels from IRIs would likely not provide useful information for students who are struggling readers and those who are highly skilled readers, and those are *exactly* the groups for whom we most need accurate data.

IRIs have been around for a long time and are frequently used. However, they have either unknown or generally poor psychometric characteristics, require an excessive amount of time to use, and may not provide useful data, especially for students with extremely low or high reading skills. Providing reading material that represents an instructional level for an individual student is a critical component of effective reading instruction. Unfortunately, IRIs cannot be effectively used to do so.

Curriculum-Based Measurement

In 1977, Deno and Mirkin proposed CBM as an alternative to IRIs in response to the factors discussed above. CBM administration involves having a student read orally from a given passage for 1 minute and recording the number of words read correctly per minute (WRCM) and the number of errors per minute (EPM). Deno and Mirkin (1977) recommended that students were reading at an instructional level if they read 30–49 WRCM for students in first through third grade, 50–99 WRCM for students in fourth grade and above, and 3–7 EPM for any grade.

There is a wealth of research regarding CBM for reading (CBM-R). Meta-analytic research found high reliability coefficients (Wayman, Wallace, Wiley, Ticha, & Espin, 2007), high correlations with norm-referenced tests (r = .60–.70; Reschly, Busch, Betts, Deno, & Long, 2009), and high correlations with performance on statewide achievement tests (r = .69; Yeo, 2009). Moreover, CBM-R data resulted in over 80% correct classification between the CBM-R data and the MAP-R measure of reading comprehension (Parker et al., in press). Thus, CBM-R seems to be an effective approach to screen students for reading difficulties. It also seems to be ideally suited to monitor reading progress from core instruction or reading interventions (Shapiro, 2011), especially given that the entire assessment would require less than 5 minutes per student. In fact, if the assessor used three passages and recorded the median score, then the assessment would require only 3 minutes and a class of 30 students could be assessed in 1.5 hours, as opposed to the 10–15 hours to conduct an IRI.

Although CBM-R data can be an important component in an assessment-to-intervention model, their utility in determining an instructional level is mostly unknown because very little research has examined this use of CBM-R data. The WRCM and EPM instructional-level criteria suggest that a student in grades 1 through 3 could read 23 of 30 (77%) words correctly to 42 of 49 (86%) words correctly, both of which do not seem to be especially indicative of proficient, or even instructional-level, reading. Moreover, the instructional-level criteria for CBM-R data were established at a school that was part of the precision teaching program being conducted in Minnesota and were not derived from research (S. L. Deno, personal communication, April 15, 2005). Recent research regarding the use of CBM-R to identify an instructional level found that the criteria recommended by Deno and Mirkin (1977) substantially overestimated the reading skills of students by identifying an instructional level when they in fact demonstrated considerable difficulty reading the passage (Parker, Burns, & McComas, 2013).

CBM has many similarities to CBA-ID, but has some fundamental differences. First, CBM is a GOM and CBA-ID is an SMM. Therefore, CBM assesses overall reading skills, but CBA-ID assesses how well a student reads a particular set of materials. CBM attempts to generalize to the broad construct of reading, but CBA-ID makes no assumptions about generalization. Data do not generalize from an individual student (i.e., one student's CBA-

ID data will not generalize to other students, even if similar in many characteristics), but they also do not generalize to the individual student (i.e., CBA-ID criteria are not assumed to generalize to any single student). Much like IRIs, CBM attempts to generalize the score to all written material. We question the generalizability of any one score to the entire universe of reading materials. When we complete a CBA-ID, we have little information about the student's overall reading skills, but we do know how well he or she will interact with the text that will be used for instruction, and we suggest that those data are what most classroom general and special education teachers really want to know.

CBM-R is a well-researched tool that is very useful for screening children and to monitor progress on a more frequent (e.g., weekly) basis because it is highly reliable, corresponds with reading comprehension, is not expensive, and does not require much time to complete. However, much like IRIs, CBM-R data do not seem to provide useful information when determining an instructional level.

Conclusion

Shapiro (2011) presents an assessment-to-intervention model that involves four steps: (1) assessing the academic environment, (2) assessing instructional placement, (3) modifying instruction, and (4) monitoring progress. Assessment data drive all four steps and different assessments serve different purposes. Thus, different assessment approaches are more relevant to certain decisions within an assessment-to-intervention/instruction framework than others. For example, CBM was noted to be the most effective assessment approach for progress monitoring, which seems to be a point of consensus in the literature (Burns, Dean, & Klar, 2004; Deno, 2003; Gresham, 2002; Shinn, Rosenfield, & Knutson, 1989), but CBA-ID may be more relevant for determining how to best modify instruction (Burns, Dean, & Klar, 2004; Shapiro, 2011). The role of IRIs in instruction seems somewhat unclear, but using CBA-ID to determine whether a particular set of materials matches student skill seems superior to making the same judgment with IRI data. Moreover, including CBA-ID along with CBM in Shapiro's integrated assessment-to-intervention model resulted in improved student outcomes (Burns, 2002; Shapiro & Ager, 1992).

ASSESSMENT PROCEDURES

Any assessment procedure should follow a standard administration because if the assessment is not administered the same way every time, then the data cannot be compared across assessments or to a criterion (Kaplan & Saccuzzo, 2001). Thus, clear directions for administration should be outlined so that the administration can be duplicated across times and potential assessment conditions (American Educational Research Association, American Psychological Association, & National Council for Measurement in Education, 1999). The administration procedures for CBM are well established (e.g., Hosp et al., 2006; Shinn, 1989), but some standardized measures, such as IRIs, include a high level of subjectivity because the assessor rates student behavior. As discussed in Chapter 1, instructional assessment (Gravois & Gickling, 2008) also has some level of subjectivity to it, but using CBA-ID within the model makes the decisions more objectively based.

Assessing the Instructional Level

There are specific administration procedures for all approaches to CBA-ID, and we discuss them in detail for reading, writing, and math in later chapters. All approaches involve using the instructional material as the assessment, directly sampling student performance, timing students as they perform the task, and comparing the data to an instructional-level criterion. Teachers have often questioned the validity of data obtained from timed assessments because they wonder about the negative consequences of having a student watch the clock as he or she works. We have several responses to that concern. First, we time the behavior for 1 minute in reading because that provides a sufficient sample of the behavior. Reading for less time (e.g., 30 seconds) did not result in reliable data but going beyond 1 minute did not improve reliability (Burns et al., 2000). Data for math and writing are converted to a per-minute metric, but students could be timed for any length and data. We suggest providing enough time for the student to complete the task (e.g., 2 minutes for single-digit multiplication and 3 minutes for writing tasks), but to limit it to the smallest interval needed to obtain a valid score. There is little benefit to providing too much time and no need to cut back time so as to pressure the student. Timing the assessment also enhances the standardization of the assessment. Finally, we just do not believe that timing is a big issue for children. We have seen countless examples that demonstrate when educators consider the timing to be routine, students follow the routine as well and become comfortable with it. There may be instances when timing is problematic for a given student (e.g., a student who stutters), and accommodations can be made on a student-by-student basis, but timing should not be an issue for a vast majority of the students.

Assessing the AR

There is one aspect of CBA-ID that remains somewhat constant across academic domains. We assess the AR for math, reading, and spelling the same way. Students can become frustrated if the task is too difficult (e.g., the student can read less than 93% of the words), but student frustration can also be the result of attempting to cover too much information. The appropriate amount of information that a student can manage and maintain while learning a particular skill/lesson is called the AR (Gravois & Gickling, 2002). Previous research found that students with documented behavioral difficulties remained engaged in task-relevant behavior during a word recognition lesson that contained 90% known words, until the lesson exceeded the students' AR, at which time the frequency of off-task behavior more than tripled (Burns & Dean, 2005a).

AR is based on the theory of retroactive cognitive interference, which occurs when students learn a new item, but then cannot recall the new item after learning a subsequent item. In other words, if you want to teach children eight items, but they can only learn four at one time, then they will learn items 1, 2, 3, and 4 with little problem, and not only will they not learn items 5, 6, 7, and 8 but attempting to teach them will cause students to forget the items that you just taught them. Have you ever seen a student who "knew it one day, but didn't know it the next day"? We believe that one reason why we see memory difficulties and inconsistent performance is that we do not frequently enough consider the limits of human memory, and assessing an AR is one way to do so.

There are potentially multiple ways to assess the AR, but we describe one method in Table 3.1 to ensure standardization. Previous research regarding the reliability and validity of AR data used the same approach (Burns, 2001; Burns & Dean, 2005a; Burns & Mosak, 2005). We begin by identifying a series of known and unknown items, which are discussed in more detail later. We need to identify five known items for children in kindergarten and younger, and eight known items for older children. We then write the known and unknown items on index cards and ask the student to correctly respond to the item (e.g., read the word, tell me the sound that the letter makes, what is 3×3). Those to which a correct response is given are counted as known items and those not correctly responded to or those to which a correct response is given after 2 seconds are counted as unknowns.

After identifying known and unknown items, the unknowns are taught using IR (Tucker, 1989), which is described in more detail in Chapter 7. First, each unknown item is presented to the student while verbally stating the correct response (e.g., "This is 4 times 4, and 4 times 4 equals 16"). Second, the student is asked to restate the correct response (e.g., "4 times 4 equals 16," correctly reading the word, or stating the sound that the letter makes). Third, the unknown item is rehearsed with IR in the following manner: first unknown, first known; first unknown, first known, second known; first unknown, first known, second known, third known; first known, second known, third known, fourth known; first known, second known, third known, fourth known, fifth known. The rehearsal would stop here for kindergarten and preschool children, but would continue in the same manner for older children until all eight known items are presented, which is considered one set.

TABLE 3.1. Procedures for Assessing an Acquisition Rate

1. Write unknown and known items on index cards.
2. Teach the words with incremental rehearsal.
3. Count any error made by the student. Errors are any incorrect response or correct responses after 2 seconds of presentation.
4. Keep adding in unknown items until the student makes three errors while rehearsing any one item. The errors may occur for a target item, a previously taught item, or a known item.
5. After the student makes three errors while rehearsing any one item (a set), stop the assessment.
6. Shuffle the items that were taught and show each one final time. Ask the student to correctly respond to each when you show the card (e.g., read the word, state the answer to a math fact, tell me what sound the letter makes). Items that are correctly responded to within 2 seconds of presentation are considered known, and those that are incorrectly responded to or correctly responded to after 2 seconds of presentation are considered unknown.
7. Count the number of known items, which equals the acquisition rate.
8. Test for retention at least 1 day later by repeating Step 6.

After completing the rehearsal pattern for the first unknown word described above (the first set), a new unknown item would be introduced (the second set), the previous unknown item is then treated as the first known item, and previous final (fifth or eighth) known item is removed from the deck. Any time a student does not correctly respond to an item written on the card, regardless if it is designated as "unknown" or "known," it is immediately corrected and counted as an error. New unknown items are added into the sequence until the student makes three errors while practicing a new item (one set). At this time, the number of unknown items successfully completed is recorded as the AR. For example, if a student rehearses the first four unknown words while making few errors, but makes three errors while completing the fifth word, his or her AR would be 4. As stated earlier, previous research found that ARs can be reliably measured ($r > .90$) for third- and fifth-grade students (Burns, 2001) and were highly correlated ($r = .70$) with a standardized norm-referenced measure of memory (Burns & Mosack, 2005). The specific steps in the assessment procedure are listed in Table 3.1 and are included in Appendix A7.

The role of ARs in intervention and instructional design are discussed in Chapter 7, but generally speaking, the AR provides an estimate about the appropriate number of new items to include when planning instruction. If a student's AR for math facts is 3, then teachers and interventionists know that providing three new math facts in any one lesson or intervention session would likely be sufficient. Teachers know that it is better to include fewer items than too many, but measuring the AR allows for precision in planning so that instructional time and student capacities can both be used to their maximum potential.

CONCLUSION

CBA-ID is an assessment approach with a specific goal. The data obtained from CBA-ID measure of reading, writing, and math can be used to design intervention and to modify instruction, and doing so results in reliable data and valid decisions. CBA-ID has limited utility for other aspects of the instructional process. For example, CBM is a stronger tool to use when monitoring student progress. The information described above demonstrates the utility of CBA-ID as an assessment tool, but it must be perceived as an assessment. Within an assessment paradigm, CBA-ID is less standardized and more informal than many measures commonly used in schools, but informal measures that directly assess the skill being taught result in data that are more useful for formative evaluation decisions. If you want to decide whether a student should be identified as having a disability, if you want to determine whether a student has passed state standards, or if you want to hold a teacher accountable for a test score, then we recommend that you use a different assessment tool than CBA-ID. However, if you want to use data to design instruction, to determine where to target your intervention efforts, or how to modify an intervention or instruction, then CBA-ID is an ideal tool to use. We next discuss how to do so in the chapters that follow.

CHAPTER 4

CBA-ID for Reading

There is considerable research regarding reading instruction and intervention. For example, the National Reading Panel (2000) summarized thousands of articles in their meta-analyses. The same is true for CBA-ID, but on a much smaller scale. Most of the CBA-ID research addresses reading, which suggests that practitioners can have considerable confidence implementing CBA-ID procedures when intervening or instructing in reading. However, there are some areas in need of additional research. Below we discuss research regarding CBA-ID for reading and the procedures to implement it, but we begin with a conversation about reading in general.

READING RESEARCH

What makes someone a proficient reader? This brief question is surprisingly controversial. Some suggest that *comprehension* and *reading* are synonymous terms, but others focus on specific skills within reading. The National Reading Panel (2000) brought some clarity to the debate by identifying five areas for effective reading instruction. The most foundational skill is phonemic awareness, which is essentially the knowledge that words are made of individual sounds that can be manipulated. Phonemic awareness is made up of blending (e.g., if you say the sounds /c/-/a/-/t/ fast, you hear the word *cat*), segmenting (When I hear the word *cat*, I hear three sounds: /c/-/a/-/t/), and manipulating (e.g., If I replace the /c/ sound in *cat* with /b/, I hear the word *bat*). Teaching how to use letters to represent sounds is called phonics and is the second component of effective reading instruction. Phonics is closely linked to phonemic awareness, but the two are often confused. Phonemic awareness is an auditory skill, which is a part of the larger idea of phonological awareness, but learning that written symbols (i.e., letters) represent the sounds is the alphabetic principle, and using letters to sound out the words is called decoding.

The National Reading Panel (2000) also identified reading fluency as an important component of reading instruction, which involves rapid and accurate reading with expression.

However, the Panel also identified fluency as often overlooked, and there has been considerably more emphasis as part of instruction since the Panel's report. Reading comprehension and vocabulary are the third and fourth components of effective reading instruction, and were identified as closely intertwined aspects of reading instruction that create thoughtful interaction between the reader and text.

Reading Fluency and Comprehension

Fast and efficient identification of words is critical because word reading is directly related to reading fluency (Carnine, Silbert, Kame'enui, & Tarver, 2004), which is directly linked to reading comprehension (Fuchs, Fuchs, Hosp, & Jenkins, 2001). In fact, recent structural equation modeling research found that reading comprehension was most affected by background knowledge and vocabulary, followed in order by correct inferences about reading, word reading skill, and strategy use (Cromley & Azevedo, 2007). In other words, background knowledge and vocabulary are critically important for comprehension, but how well students comprehend what they read has more to do with how well they read the words than how well they apply comprehension strategies. That is likely important because comprehension strategies are often the first intervention attempted when a student struggles with comprehension, but that might miss the target for many students.

Reading fluency has also been shown to be important to comprehension in second grade (Berninger, Abbott, Vermeulen, & Fulton, 2006; Schwanenflugel et al., 2006), and second grade is when children transition from beginning reading skills to reading fluency (Chall, 1983). In fact, differences in oral reading fluency (ORF) between normal and struggling readers occur as early as first grade (Speece & Ritchey, 2005).

CBA-ID focuses on basic skills such as fluency and decoding, but that is likely appropriate given that many struggling readers struggle to break the code (National Reading Panel, 2000). Fluency-building interventions lead to strong effects for comprehension (Burns, Dean, & Foley, 2004; Therrien, 2004). It could be that children who slowly decode words one sound at a time will not be able to retain the meaning of words they have read after completing a sentence or paragraph and that automatic word recognition is needed in order for the reader's finite attention and processing resources to be devoted to comprehension of the text (LaBerge & Samuels, 1974). Some argue that language is a causal mechanism for comprehension, and oral language comprehension is more closely related to reading comprehension than ORF, but ORF does account for unique variance in reading comprehension assessments (Spear-Swerling, 2006). Moreover, previous research has effectively used reading fluency interventions to increase reading comprehension (Alber-Morgan, Ramp, Anderson, & Martin, 2007; Burns, Dean, & Foley, 2004; Freeland, Skinner, Jackson, McDaniel, & Smith, 2000; Therrien, 2004),

First and second graders needed to read about 60 WRCM in order for comprehension to occur. Third and fourth graders needed to read at about 50 WRCM.

We have twice conducted research in which we artificially slowed down student ORF to measure the effect on comprehension. We presented a series of reading passages to 84 first- and second-grade students, and 49 third- and fourth-grade students with increasing percentages of scrambled words (0%, 10%, 20%, and 30%) and asked them to read the passages orally and answer comprehension questions. Reading fluency and comprehension both significantly decreased as the percentage of words increased, but we also found that first and second graders needed to read about 60 WRCM in order for comprehension to occur (Burns, Kwoka, et al., 2011), and third and fourth graders needed to read at about 50 WRCM to comprehend their reading (Burns et al., 2002).

When we consult with teachers about students with reading difficulties, we frequently hear that the student "does not understand a word that he reads." However, we have discovered that the reason he does not understand a word is that he is not reading the words. Most of the time that we assess a student with reported comprehension difficulties, he or she reads less than 50 WRCM from grade-level material, which suggests that the comprehension deficit is really just a fluency deficit in disguise. When we have the student read from instructional-level text, or we remediate the fluency deficit, then the comprehension problem disappears.

CBA-ID focuses on fluency by finding the percentage of words read correctly, but as stated above, fluent word reading is necessary for comprehension. Moreover, how accurately a student reads the text is closely linked to comprehension, even after factoring out listening comprehension (Spooner, Baddeley, & Gathercole, 2004). Valencia and Riddle Buly (2004) examined assessment data for 108 struggling readers to identify six distinct profiles, all but one that involved poor accuracy, fluency, or both. Therefore, most students who struggle with reading will require increased accuracy or rate with which they read the words. Teachers and school psychologists are encouraged to ask students comprehension question about what they read within a CBA-ID, but the procedures focus on percentage of words read correctly.

Decoding and Reading

The Early Child Longitudinal Study (ECLS) suggests that by the spring of their kindergarten year, most students demonstrate letter recognition skills (94%), can discriminate between beginning sounds (94%) and ending sounds of words (70%), begin to apply the alphabetic principle (92%), and in some cases even begin to establish sight-word recognition (14%) (Walston & West, 2004). The proportion of students with sight-word proficiency in first grade improves from 26 to 78%. Thus, first-grade students have at least started to establish a bank of automatic words, but have also began to establish phonemic awareness (knowledge that words are made of sounds that can be manipulated) and word-attack skills. However, students who struggle with these foundational skills experience substantial difficulties learning how to read (Stanovich, 1986).

The simple view of reading states that reading comprises two aspects: word recognition and language comprehension (Gough & Tunmer, 1986). There is considerable empirical support for the simple view of reading, especially for targeting interventions based on the dichotomy (Catts, Adlof, & Weismer, 2006). However, recent research found that children with comprehension difficulties benefited from instruction in code-based aspects of reading such as decoding, phonemic awareness, or fluency (Tan, Wheldhall, Madelaine, & Lee, 2009). Early interventions in critical skill areas, such as decoding, are likely to reduce the incidence of low academic achievement (Jenkins & O'Connor, 2002; Schatschneider & Torgesen, 2004; Torgesen, 2002), which suggests that interventions that occur by the second grade have a higher likelihood of leading to successful comprehension (Juel, 1988; Snow, Burns, & Griffin, 1998).

Much like our experience with referrals for reading comprehension problems, we often see teachers implementing fluency interventions when phonics skills were the appropriate target. Some have suggested that poor readers need increased independent reading as an intervention (Allington, 2009). We agree that all children need practice reading connected text, and struggling readers need additional practice. However, connected text practice alone will not be sufficient if the student struggles to decode the basic sounds. Pikulski and Chard (2005) reviewed research regarding reading fluency and Ehri's (1998) stages of reading development to conclude that students should be taught common word parts and decoding strategies before they use text to practice strategic reading to build speed or engage in repeated reading procedures. Therefore, it may be appropriate to take a step back and intervene with basic decoding skills before engaging in fluency-building skills.

> All children need practice reading connected text, and struggling readers need additional practice. However, connected text practice alone will not be sufficient if the student struggles to decode the basic sounds.

Reading Interventions

The five areas identified by the National Reading Panel can serve as a heuristic to target reading interventions. The five areas could be conceptualized as code focused (phonemic awareness, phonics, and fluency) and meaning focused (vocabulary and comprehension), and follow a developmental pattern among struggling readers in which phonemic awareness leads to decoding, which leads to fluency, which leads to comprehension (Berninger et al., 2006). Proficient readers may actually be more of a puzzle than struggling readers because good readers may use different strategies or use other cues to comprehend the text, but struggling readers tend to be much more sequential in their development. For example, although we occasionally find students who do not demonstrate sufficient fluency and who comprehend what they read, research is clear that teachers significantly overestimate the frequency of so-called word callers (Hamilton & Shinn, 2003; Meisinger, Bradley, Schwanenflugel, & Kuhn, 2010; Meisinger, Bradley, Schwanenflugel, Kuhn, & Morris, 2009). If a student comprehends what he or she reads without sufficient speed, then most teachers are not concerned because comprehension is the ultimate goal. However, if a student struggles with comprehension and fluency, then we have to screen decoding skills to be sure where to start our intervention efforts.

Although quality instruction should address both code and meaning, it is likely that children younger than 9 years old would demonstrate more deficits in code issues because many of the reading deficits in kindergarten to first grades are related to phonemic awareness difficulties, first to second grade are phonetic skills, and third grade are reading fluency deficits (Snow et al., 1998). Although reading comprehension is the ultimate goal of reading instruction, the code-focused skills are prerequisites to developing literacy skills and should probably be the focus of most intervention efforts among students in kindergarten through second grade.

CBA-ID PROCEDURES

CBA-ID for reading is usually conducted in a one-on-one assessment session. There are techniques to collect the data quickly and efficiently, which are discussed in Chapter 7, but below we discuss the basic procedures for contextual reading, conducting survey-level assessments, word searches, letter sounds, and highly decodable words.

Contextual Reading

Procedures for CBA-ID were initially developed for contextual reading, which remains the most common application. The assessment begins by identifying the reading material to use. Teachers and school psychologists should focus on material to be used for immediate upcoming reading instruction. The material should include sufficient text to sample the behavior, but unlike other assessment approaches, it may take multiple pages to assess the skill. Therefore, the assessor should identify enough pages from the upcoming instructional material to engage the reader for at least 1 minute, which would likely be 100 to 150 words.

Once the material is identified, the assessor then photocopies the pages to serve as a testing protocol. However, the actual instructional materials are used for the assessment. If the student is going to be reading from a reading basal, then he or she is asked to read from the basal as the assessment. Previous research found that students who are struggling readers perform differently when presented with a book as opposed to typed probes (Lagrou, Burns, Mizerek, & Mosack, 2006). Therefore, CBA-ID uses authentic materials to assess reading to most closely match the instructional task. Some might object to providing cues such as pictures because doing so might not provide a pure measure of reading. Remember that CBA-ID does not measure how well a child reads; it measures how well the child can read a specific book, page, materials, and so on.

Once the material is identified and photocopied, place the book/page/materials in front of the student, then say to him or her: "Start right here and please read this out loud so that I can hear you. Do your very best reading. If you come to a word that you don't know, I'll tell it to you. Keep reading until I tell you to stop. Ready? Begin." Start the timer and follow along as the student reads to record errors. Any word that is not read correctly within 2 seconds is counted as an error, which might include omissions, mispronunciations (allowing for local dialects), or correct reading after 2 seconds. Be sure to tell the student the correct pronunciation so that errors will not interfere with comprehension.

At the end of 1 minute, tell the student to stop. We time the student for 1 minute so that we can get a measure of reading fluency, but also because 1 minute seems to provide a sufficient sample of the behavior to provide reliable data. Count the number of words read correctly, divide by the total number of words (words correctly read plus number of errors), and multiply by 100. Compare that percentage to the criterion of 93–97%. If the percentage falls within 93–97%, then the passage represents an instructional level. More challenging materials (less than 93% correct) represents a frustration level, and more than 97% correct represents an independent level.

We recommend repeating this process two additional times and selecting the median. Practitioners could determine the appropriate reading target (i.e., material to be used for reading instruction) and randomly select portions of it. For example, if the next story from the reading basal is 10 pages long, then the even numbered pages could be randomly selected so that the student would read pages 216–217, 220–221, and 224–225. The median percentage of the three is used to evaluate the instructional level.

After conducting the assessment, teachers and school psychologists are encouraged to ask reading comprehension questions. Day and Park (2005) describe six types of comprehension questions including (1) literal—surface-level recall of facts in the text, (2) reorganization—combing different aspects of the text for additional understanding, (3) inference—using background knowledge to answer questions that are not explicitly stated in the text, (4) prediction—using both background knowledge and knowledge of the passage to determine what will likely happen next, (5) evaluation—judge some aspect of the text, and (6) personal response—readers respond with their own feelings about what they read that can reflect literal understanding but must relate to the text. Comprehension assessments should tap all six types of questions, which suggests that the student should answer at least 6 to 12 questions for each passage.

There are several types of questions that are appropriate for assessing comprehension, including true and false, multiple choice, matching, and short answer (Linn & Miller, 2005). True and false, and matching are simplistic approaches that should be used to assess low-level comprehension such as literal and reorganization. Multiple-choice items can be used to assess low-level comprehension, but can also be used to assess inferencing, and prediction. Finally, short answer is the easiest to construct and is the most commonly used approach (Linn & Miller, 2005). A short-answer format can assess literal, reorganization, inference, and prediction with little preparation, but short-answer questions are almost required to assess evaluation and personal response. Because the instructional level for drill tasks (including comprehension questions) is 85–90%, the student should correctly answer at least 85% of the questions correctly. However, the comprehension data are used for instructional purposes and are not used to primarily judge the instructional level.

Survey-Level Assessments

Informal reading inventories are based on the idea of a survey-level assessment in which easier or more difficult passages are presented until the highest level that represents an instructional level is identified. The shortcomings of informal reading inventories are discussed in Chapter 3, but survey-level assessments may be helpful and are described as an important part of an assessment-to-intervention model (Shapiro, 2011).

As discussed in Chapter 7, the teacher may choose to start with a grade-level probe or to estimate the level that may represent an instructional level. If the percentage of known words for that passage is less than 93%, then easier passages are used until the student correctly reads 93%. If the student correctly reads more than 97% of the words, then more difficult passages would be administered until the percentage falls within 93–97% correct. Although this approach is commonly used, it is often interpreted with faulty instructional-level criteria or is over interpreted to generalize to all reading material. Remember, these data only generalize to the material being sampled and not to reading in general, which means that practitioners may have to complete multiple CBA-ID in order to identify enough reading material to use for reading instruction.

Word Search

If the reading material to be used for instruction is too difficult (i.e., frustration level), then practitioners could use easier material or could preteach enough words to facilitate an instructional level (see Chapter 7). Gravois and Gickling (2002) provide a description of how to identify unknown words to preteach through a process called a word search. The reading material is surveyed by pointing to words that the teacher or school psychologist believes the student could not read. The student is asked to read each word within 2 seconds by saying, "We are going to read some words. Please read the words that I point to. Some will be harder and some will be easier. Do your very best to read each word. Any questions? Let's start." Then point to the first word and say "What is this word?" Those that were correctly read within the 2-second limit are considered known and those that were incorrectly read or correctly read beyond 2 seconds are considered unknown.

> **If the reading material to be used for instruction is too difficult (i.e., frustration level), then practitioners could use easier material or could preteach enough words to facilitate an instructional level.**

Keep pointing to words until enough unknown words are identified to preteach while staying within the student's AR. Record the words that the student does not correctly read within 2 seconds. However, as also recommended by Gravois and Gickling (2008), every third word pointed to should be one that the student could likely read easily in order to ensure that enough known words are found and to keep the activity from being too frustrating.

Letter Sounds

Teachers need to know if students need additional work with decoding and which letter sounds to teach to the student. Therefore, a quick 1-minute assessment of letter sounds can be quite beneficial. We suggest a two-part process. Start by assessing students with low-frequency highly decodable words. Various nonsense and pseudoword measures can be strong indicators of decoding skills, but teachers occasionally object to use of artificial words. Research suggests that teachers' concerns about using pseudoword assessments are not well founded (see Chapter 7), but they can be easily accommodated by using words that follow typical decoding patterns and are low frequency.

Practitioners can find several free lists of highly-decodable and low-frequency words at *www.cehd.umn.edu/reading/PRESS/docs/assessments/06.Kindergarten-Word-Identification-Fluency-General-Outcome-Measure.pdf*, and as shown in Figure 4.1. Present the student with the list of words and say to the student, "Here is a list of words. Start at the top [point to the first word], and read them out loud going this way [point left to right]. Do your very best reading and try all of the words. Keep reading until I tell you to stop. Any questions? Begin."

Start the timer and record sounds that the student does not read correctly by placing a slash through them on the assessment protocol in Appendix A. After 1 minute, say "Stop" and count the number of sounds read correctly and errors for each line. Divide the total number of sounds read correctly by the total number of sounds attempted (Read Correctly/[Read Correctly + Errors]) and multiply by 100 to get a percentage. If the student reads at least 85% of the sounds correctly, then he or she likely demonstrates sufficient basic decoding skills. However, if the student does not read at least 85% of the sounds correctly, then he or she likely needs additional support in decoding and the teacher or school psychologist should assess specific sounds.

In order to determine which sounds to target, present the student with a list of letter and letter combinations (e.g., *ch, th, sh*) that can be easily created, taken from letter–sound fluency measures, or created from websites such as *www.interventioncentral.com*. Present the student with the list of letters and letter combinations and say to the student, "Here is a list of letters. Start at the top [point to first letter–letter combination], and say what each letter says. Read them out loud going this way [point left to right]. Do your very best and try all of the letters. Keep going until I tell you to stop. Any questions? Begin."

Start the timer and record sounds that the student does not read correctly by placing a slash through them on the assessment protocol. After 1 minute, say "Stop" and count the number of sounds read correctly and errors for each line. Divide the total number of sounds read correctly by the total number of sounds attempted (Read Correctly/[Read Correctly + Errors]) and multiply by 100 to get a percentage. Reading 85–90% of the sounds correctly represents an instructional level, but more importantly, the incorrect letter sounds can be identified to teach to the student.

wig	jam	yep
gap	sup	gad
bop	yup	bud
cop	sap	hog

FIGURE 4.1. Sample low-frequency but highly decodable words.

CONCLUSION

As stated earlier, there is a great deal of research regarding CBA-ID for reading and the procedures are easily implemented with a photocopy, a writing utensil, and a calculator. Thus, any general education/special education teacher or school psychologist can collect the data with little training. Moreover, the data from CBA-ID are easily translated into interventions. We next discuss procedures for math and writing, and then how to use the data to drive instruction and intervention.

CHAPTER 5

CBA-ID for Math

Formative evaluation is especially important for mathematics (National Council of Teachers of Mathematics, 2000, 2006; National Mathematics Advisory Panel, 2008), and should suggest specific objectives and/or items that need to be taught and how to best teach them (Stiggins, 2005). As discussed in Chapter 3, CBA-ID is an effective approach for formative evaluation because the data directly inform what to teach and how to teach it.

Math proficiency comprises both conceptual understanding and procedural fluency (Kilpatrick, Swafford, & Finell, 2001), both of which should be assessed with CBA-ID to design intervention and instruction. Conceptual knowledge is the understanding of the relationships that underlie mathematics problems, and procedural knowledge is the understanding of the rules and steps to actually solve the problems (Hiebert & Lefevre, 1986). A recent meta-analysis found a negligible effect for conceptual math interventions, and reported that conceptual math interventions "present a complex puzzle of findings, open to multiple interpretations" (Baker, Gersten, & Lee, 2002, p. 66). However, it could be that one reason why the conceptual interventions were not more effective was because they did not address the student deficit. Students with math difficulties frequently struggle to rapidly solve basic math facts (Geary, Hoard, Byrd-Craven, Nugent, & Numtee, 2007; Hanich, Jordan, Kaplan, & Dick, 2001), and require additional support in procedural issues or practice completing basic facts to increase fluency. Only a portion of students who struggle with math require a conceptual intervention (e.g., using math manipulatives to demonstrate the problem). In our experience, teachers tend to pull out the manipulative objects whenever a student struggles with math in order to reteach the concept, but that is often not what the student needs. In our research regarding conceptual understanding interventions, we have had great difficulty finding students who do not adequately understand the concept; most get the underlying ideas, but they cannot complete the procedures. Think of the student who can use blocks to determine that 5 objects and 6

> **Students with math difficulties frequently struggle to rapidly solve basic math facts.**

objects make 11 objects when put together, but cannot solve the written problem $5 + 6 = ?$ Below, we discuss how to use CBA-ID to assess both types of skills.

MATH PROCEDURES

Conceptual knowledge is the foundation on which math skills are built, but many students struggle with completing the computation despite understanding the underlying concept. We discuss CBA-ID for procedures first because it is probably more commonly used and is more straightforward. CBA-ID looks very much like curriculum-based measurement (CBM) when assessing math procedures. The fundamental difference between CBA-ID and CBM is the scope of the assessment. CBM is a global outcome measure that assesses overall math skills, and CBA-ID is a subskill mastery measure that assesses specific skills and objectives. However, the two assessment approaches are similar in one respect for math: they are less directly representative of the curriculum. With reading, the assessment stimuli for CBA-ID are the actual book or reading material used for instruction, but we often develop probes for math assessments within CBA-ID. If we are assessing objectives like single-digit multiplication, then the assessment clearly aligns with curricular objectives, but it may be more representative of the curriculum than a direct sampling of it.

CBA-ID begins for math by selecting the objective to assess. We discuss selecting objectives to assess this in great detail in Chapter 7. For now, we simply state that the assessment begins by selecting an objective from the scope and sequence of the math curriculum. Teacher and school psychologists can then use math assessment provided by the curriculum if appropriate, or can create their own with a web-based system (e.g., *www.mathfactscafe. com*), or just design the assessment themselves.

We rely heavily on CBM research when designing a CBA-ID probe for math. The math CBM probe should contain at least 25 problems depending on the curriculum difficulty, and the order of the problems randomly determined. Moreover, the number of items is not a hard-and-fast rule and school psychologists should ensure that enough items are presented to adequately sample the skill given the individual student's proficiency.

After constructing the probes, students are given 2–4 minutes to complete as many items as they can. Recent research has supported allowing 4 minutes to complete the task (Christ, Johnson-Gros, & Hintze, 2005), but some recommend allowing 2 minutes for students in grades 1 through 3 (Aimsweb, 2006). Administration consists of handing the student the sheet to be completed and providing directions: "Please write the answers to some problems. Look at each problem carefully before answering it. Start with the first problem and work across the page. Try all of the problems, but place an X over problems that you do not know how to do. Keep working until I tell you to stop" (Shinn & Shinn, 2004). After 2 or 4 minutes the administration stops and the probe is collected for scoring. CBA-ID probes can be used to assess individual students, but can also be used for an entire class, as we discuss in Chapter 7.

CBA-ID math is not assessed with percentage of items correct like reading, but instead are scored in digits correct per minute (DCPM). Accuracy data are not reliable enough to use for math, but fluency data are reliable and correlate well with other math measures (Burns et al., 2006). Most teachers would see $3 \times 5 = 15$ and $4 \times 5 = 20$ as two correct out of two (100%), but with digits correct, the student would receive credit for two digits for each answer (1 and 5, and 2 and 0), which would be four out of four. The following set of answers $3 \times 5 = 18$, $4 \times 7 = 25$, and $4 \times 5 = 20$ would be four out of six digits correct instead of one out of three. The student would receive credit for the "1" in 18 because that digit is correct and in the correct place, and the "2" in the second problem would also receive credit, but the "8" and "5," respectively, would be scored as incorrect. The student would also receive two out of two for the answer 20 because both digits are correct and in the correct place.

Digits correct are also scored in the critical processes of a problem with placeholders counting as correct digits. The problems shown in Figure 5.1 have 17 possible digits correct each rather than 5, with 3 in the first row, 4 in the second row, 5 in the third row, and 5 in the answer line. Thus, the student would receive credit for one digit correct for the 0 placeholder in the second row and two digits correct for the double 0 placeholder in the third row. The student in the second example in Figure 5.1 multiplied 5×5 and mistakenly recorded 23, which resulted in not earning credit for the "3" in the first row or the final answer (15 out of 17 correct).

In order to determine DCPM, the total number of digits correct in the probe is divided by the length of the administration (i.e., 60 digits correct in a 4-minute administration would result in 15 DCPM). The data are then compared with fluency criteria for an instructional level. Deno and Mirkin (1977) recommended that 21–40 DCPM represented an instructional level for students in first through third grade and 41–80 DCPM for fourth through 12th graders. The Deno and Mirkin (1977) standards are often cited, but are not

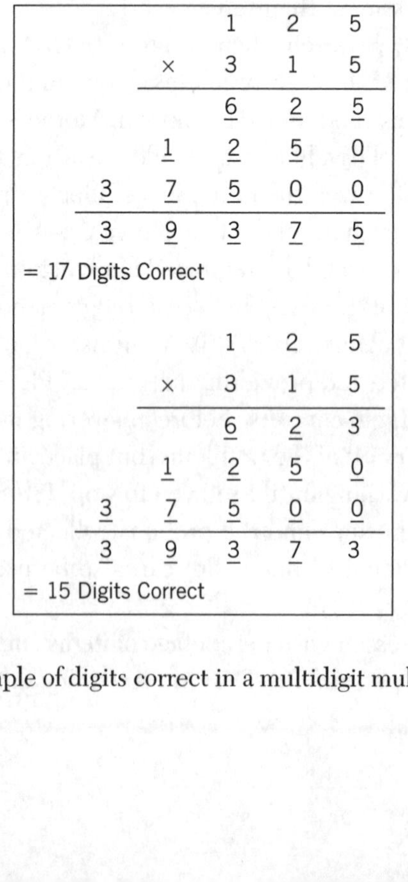

$$
\begin{array}{rrrr}
 & 1 & 2 & 5 \\
\times & 3 & 1 & 5 \\
\hline
 & \underline{6} & \underline{2} & \underline{5} \\
1 & \underline{2} & \underline{5} & \underline{0} \\
\underline{3} \quad \underline{7} & \underline{5} & \underline{0} & \underline{0} \\
\hline
\underline{3} \quad \underline{9} & \underline{3} & \underline{7} & \underline{5} \\
\end{array}
$$

= 17 Digits Correct

$$
\begin{array}{rrrr}
 & 1 & 2 & 5 \\
\times & 3 & 1 & 5 \\
\hline
 & \underline{6} & \underline{2} & 3 \\
1 & \underline{2} & \underline{5} & \underline{0} \\
\underline{3} \quad \underline{7} & \underline{5} & \underline{0} & \underline{0} \\
\hline
\underline{3} \quad \underline{9} & \underline{3} & \underline{7} & 3 \\
\end{array}
$$

= 15 Digits Correct

FIGURE 5.1. Example of digits correct in a multidigit multiplication problem.

based on research. A recent study found empirically derived instructional-level criteria of 14–31 DCPM for second and third graders, and 24–49 DCPM for older students (Burns et al., 2006). Scores below the lowest end of the instructional-level range fall within the frustration level and suggest that the skill is too difficult for the child, and those that exceed the highest score of the instructional-level range fall within the independent range.

> **A recent study found empirically derived instructional level criteria of 14–31 DCPM for second and third graders, and 24–49 DCPM for older students.**

Fluency data obtained from CBA-ID result in reliable decision making, as long as they are based on the research-based criteria of 14–31 DCPM and 24–49 DCPM. Decisions made with the Deno and Mirkin (1977) criteria were less stable, which could result in inconsistent or erroneous decision making. Moreover, interventions used for students in the frustration-level range, according to the empirically derived criteria, that focused on initial acquisition of the skill were more effective than those that focused on building fluency, but fluency-based interventions were more effective for students who scored in the instructional-level range (Burns, Codding, Boice, & Lukito, 2010). Therefore, assessments of procedural skills with CBA-ID are useful data for designing math interventions.

MATH CONCEPTS

Although procedural information is important for problem analysis of math difficulties, interventions for children with more severe difficulties cannot rely solely on procedural indicators. Many procedural errors are easily observed in students' written work (Rivera & Bryant, 1992), but conceptual errors are often difficult to observe through completed problems (LeFevre et al., 2006). Teachers and school psychologists can assess conceptual understanding by either asking students to judge whether items are correctly completed or by asking students about errors (Canobi, Reeve, & Pattison, 2002, 2003; Cowan, Dowker, Christakis, & Bailey, 1996). We discuss both approaches within a CBA-ID framework below.

Judging Correct Items

An efficient manner to assess conceptual understanding is to provide the student two examples of the same mathematical equation, one that is correct and one that contains an error, along with a pictorial representation of the problem and asking the student to select the correct choice. We previously used a similar approach to differentiate procedural and conceptual difficulties and matched the intervention based on the data, which resulted in increased math skills once the intervention was correctly matched (Burns, 2011).

CBA-ID for math concepts begins by creating a sheet that contains equations and pictures like the examples in Figure 5.2. A complete assessment sheet is included in Appendix B. Present the student with a sheet that represents the target problems and say to the student, "Here are some math problems. Each problem has two number sentences/equations and a picture. Circle the number sentence/equation for each problem that goes with the

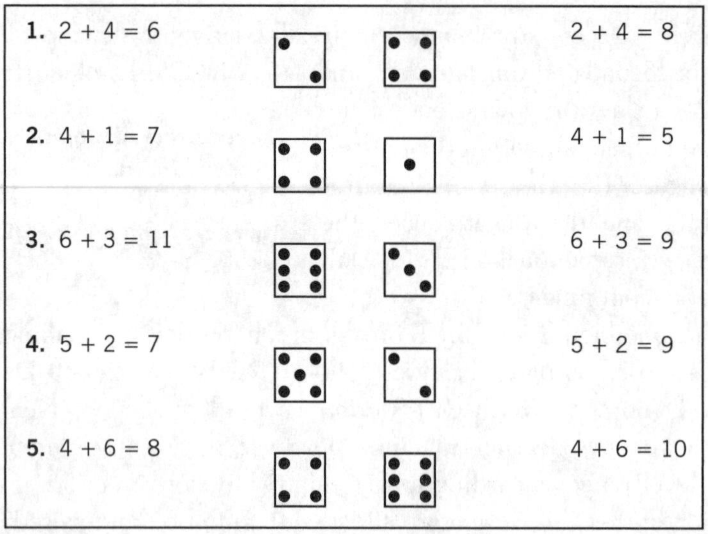

1. 2 + 4 = 6	2 + 4 = 8
2. 4 + 1 = 7	4 + 1 = 5
3. 6 + 3 = 11	6 + 3 = 9
4. 5 + 2 = 7	5 + 2 = 9
5. 4 + 6 = 8	4 + 6 = 10

FIGURE 5.2. Sample conceptual understanding assessment items.

picture. Any questions? Begin." Use the word *number sentence* for younger students and *equation* for older students.

The assessment is not timed because accuracy rather than fluency is important for conceptual understanding. The data for the conceptual understanding assessment is the percentage of correctly completed items. Because an instructional level for drill tasks like this is 85–90% (Chapter 2), a student who does not correctly complete at least 85% is likely not understanding the underlying concept. In our experience, the students either answer 90% or higher correctly, or answer about 50% correctly. We rarely see between 50 and 90% correct. If the student does not demonstrate sufficient conceptual understanding, then a conceptual intervention should be implemented.

> **If the student does not demonstrate sufficient conceptual understanding, then a conceptual intervention should be implemented.**

Teachers and school psychologists should be sure to directly sample a specific objective for the assessment. Remember, CBA-ID is a subskill mastery measure, not a general outcome measure (Chapter 3), and should not be used to assess overall math skills. In addition, be sure to include enough problems to sample the behavior, which is probably 20 items. One advantage of this approach is that the sheet can be handed out and conducted in a group administration. Research on the psychometrics of this approach is ongoing, but initial data suggest sufficient interobserver agreement and reliability (Burns, 2011).

Interviewing about Errors

Although the brief assessment described above can be helpful, it is somewhat limited in scope and likely more appropriate for students in early elementary grades. An interview protocol might be more appropriate for assessing conceptual understanding of older students. We modified the questions to create the five questions presented in Table 5.1 and in the assessment form presented in Appendix C. The assessment begins by providing the student with two sample target items and saying, "Draw a picture that shows each of these two problems. Then, use the picture to solve the problems. I will ask you some questions about your work when you are finished. Any questions? Please begin." Again, this assessment is not timed.

After the student completes the task, he or she is asked the questions presented in Table 5.1. The student's responses are scored according to the criteria presented in Table 5.2 and Appendix C. Each item is scored with a 4-point rubric based on Van de Walle and Lovin (2006). A score of a 1 indicates the student demonstrated unsatisfactory knowledge of the item, a 2 equals partial demonstration of the item, a 3 indicates adequate understanding to accomplish the objective, and a 4 indicates full accomplishment of the item. Scores could range from 0 to 24. The instructional level for drill tasks is 85–90%. Thus, a score of 20 or higher is needed to suggest that the student has adequate conceptual understanding. A sample problem, student responses, and completed scoring sheet are included in Appendix C.

Reliability estimates for the interview approach suggest acceptable reliability. Cronbach's alpha from previous research was .87 for the six items. The total scores between the two sets of scores were correlated and resulted in a high coefficient of .95. Moreover, the total number of times the data fell within the same category (low conceptual knowledge or acceptable conceptual knowledge) for each scorer was divided by the total number of participants and multiplied by 100. The resulting 100% agreement suggested adequate interobserver agreement.

Together, the various approaches to CBA-ID with math indicate the data can be used to target intervention across a range of ages and curricular objectives. In the interview approach, research demonstrates that categorical data can be interpreted with confidence, which means a student at the frustration level does struggle to understand the conceptual demands of the task. Again, the usefulness of

> **CBA-ID helps educators target interventions that will improve the student's conceptual misunderstandings.**

TABLE 5.1. Questions Used to Conduct a Conceptual Understanding Interview

- *Question 1.* "How did you figure out this problem?"
- *Question 2.* "How did you find the answer?"
- *Question 3.* "What do [point to pictures/objects] you mean and how did they help you solve the problem?"
- *Question 4.* "Tell me what you were thinking in your head when you were doing this."
- *Question 5.* "How did you check your answer to see if it was correct?"
  - *Follow-up 1.* "Please tell me more about what you did so I can understand you better."
  - *Follow-up 2.* "I never thought about it that way. Can you tell me more?"

TABLE 5.2. Scoring Criteria for a Conceptual Understanding Interview

1. Counts with understanding.
2. Understands the number sign.
3. Understands the facts of adding/subtracting or multiplication/division of whole numbers.
4. Correctly uses the visual model (i.e., there was a correct relationship between the diagram that the student created and the problem).
5. Uses an identifiable strategy.
6. Answers the problem correctly.

accurate CBA-ID data is that a student in the "frustration" level has direct implications for instruction. Unlike other forms of assessment that require higher degrees of inference (Christ, 2008), CBA-ID helps educators target interventions that will improve the student's conceptual misunderstandings. If conceptual understanding is not strong, modeling, visuals, and immediate feedback during the math exercises will be helpful for the student, whereas if conceptual understanding is sufficiently strong, intervention can focus on improving proficiency with which students complete the skills.

CONCLUSION

The level of student math proficiency is closely linked to successful employment for various occupations (Saffer, 1999), but math research has been considerably less prominent than reading research over the past decade. Various policy groups have not been able to agree on what constitutes effective math instruction, but they all agree that assessment and data-based instruction are critically important (National Council of Teachers of Mathematics, 2000, 2006; National Mathematics Advisory Panel, 2008). CBA-ID is not as familiar to most teachers and school psychologists as CBM and other assessment approaches, but the resulting data can be useful in designing interventions, whereas other types of data only suggest who needs intervention and if the intervention is working.

CHAPTER 6

CBA-ID for Early Writing

Writing has a history of being neglected from the educational reform agenda (National Commission on Writing, 2003), but that appears to be changing because the Common Core State Standards (CCSS) include benchmarks for student writing skills across grade levels (National Governors Association & Council of State School Officers, 2010). Although the inclusion of writing in nationwide standards is a good first step, educators charged with using the standards to guide instruction and actually improve student outcomes will require effective intervention approaches to meet the needs of struggling students and instructionally relevant assessment to accurately target those interventions.

Trends from national data highlight the challenge in improving writing outcomes. The most recent National Assessment of Educational Progress found an increase in the number of students reaching basic levels of writing performance but no increase in students meeting proficiency levels (Salahu-Din, Persky, & Miller, 2008). Failure to increase the number of students reaching proficient writing levels is concerning because strong writing skills predict a variety of positive outcomes, from subsequent learning (Bangert-Drowns, Hurley, & Wilkinson, 2004) to better employment prospects (National Commission on Writing, 2004, 2005). These positive outcomes exist because writing is a basic mode of communication in today's society. Individuals who can write well can communicate their thoughts and ideas effectively, which is vital to everything from responding to test questions to performing in the workplace.

Early intervention can help prevent subsequent writing difficulties (Graham, Harris, & Larsen, 2001) and is therefore an important period in which to identify effective assessment and intervention practices. The challenge with intervening early is that students rarely have the exact same writing need. Johnny may need intervention so he can write words with common spelling patterns. Susan may need intervention to improve fluent (and accurate) produc-

> **The challenge with intervening early is that students rarely have the exact same writing need.**

tion of text. Eduardo may need intervention to organize what he wants to write and complete a brief paragraph that makes sense. Depending on the students' main writing deficit, intervention would clearly take on a different emphasis. The difficulty lies in accurately identifying those needs.

USING THE INSTRUCTIONAL LEVEL IN WRITING

As discussed in Chapters 1 and 2, CBA-ID uses assessment data to help determine the nature of intervention. CBA-ID in writing incorporates the same general principles as other academic domains: A curricular task is used to provide assessment information in order to identify the instructional needs of the student and target a maximally effective intervention (Gickling et al., 1989). In writing, however, CBA-ID needs to be operationalized somewhat differently.

The idea of an instructional level is central to CBA-ID because it produces strong positive outcomes for students (e.g., Burns, 2002, 2007; Burns, Codding, et al., 2010; Shapiro & Ager, 1992; Treptow et al., 2007), and because all teachers intuitively strive to teach students at their appropriate level of challenge. The difference when using the instructional level in writing is that the task of writing requires students to *produce* something on blank paper. The product is almost entirely dependent on the student's performance; the teacher simply provides a writing task (e.g., write a sentence, create a story). This is different from other domains, where the task is to *respond* to instructional materials that can be controlled at the teacher's discretion. For example, reading material from an easier text can be provided or single-digit multiplication problems can be assigned instead of multidigit problems. In reading and math, CBA-ID data can be used by educators to make instructional changes in material. Similar changes cannot be made to instructional material in writing, which means CBA-ID data need to be used differently.

The instructional level in writing is used to inform instructional changes in intervention strategies given the student's present performance. For example, if CBA-ID data indicate the student's writing performance is in the frustration level, the student cannot produce text proficiently enough to benefit from independent practice of writing. The student struggles to accurately spell words or produce written letters and/or sentences to the point that the act of writing is too difficult to be performed independently. The student needs research-based intervention strategies that model and explicitly teach spelling and/or handwriting skills. Another student's CBA-ID data may indicate writing performance at the independent level, which means the student can spell and produce accurate letters and sentences

> If CBA-ID data indicate the student's writing performance is in the frustration level, the student cannot produce text proficiently enough to benefit from independent practice of writing.

sufficiently well that his or her writing difficulties may be related to an inability to plan, organize, and revise his or her writing product. A third student may have CBA-ID data indicating writing performance within the instructional level, and would benefit from instruction that helps him or her become more proficient at producing writing so that the student has the mental resources to think about planning, organizing, and revising his or her writing. It is no doubt an easy exercise for educators to think of students who would fit each of these categories.

The CBA-ID data for writing have promising psychometric characteristics that indicate the data can be interpreted with at least as much confidence as data produced by costly, more time-consuming standardized assessments (Parker et al., 2011). This means that CBA-ID data indicating a student's skills are below, within, or above an instructional level can be considered trustworthy. In addition, CBA-ID procedures have also been integrated within a comprehensive assessment framework (Parker, Burns, McMaster, & Shapiro, 2012). It integrates CBA-ID into a well-researched and well-conceptualized theory of skill development known as the instructional hierarchy (Haring & Eaton, 1978). This framework provides clear suggestions for making instructional changes that correspond to the CBA-ID data, and it is described with greater detail later in this chapter.

PROCEDURES TO COLLECT CBA-ID DATA IN WRITING

The procedures for conducting CBA-ID with writing begin with identifying an appropriate curricular task that can be measured efficiently and accurately. McMaster and colleagues have engaged in a line of research that produced curriculum-based measures for young writers (CBM-W; McMaster et al., 2011). The most promising of these measures include several picture–word combinations that serve as a writing prompt for students to create complete sentences (see Figure 6.1 for an example). Administration begins with a brief explanation and model of how to create a sentence. Then the student is given 3 minutes to write as many

bake

coat

FIGURE 6.1. Two sample picture–word items from a curriculum-based measure for writing (McMaster, Du, & Petursdottir, 2009).

accurate sentences as possible in response to the picture–word combinations. CBM-W can be scored to produce a variety of metrics, including the number of words written, number of correctly spelled words, and number of correct word sequences (CWS). The number of CWS consists of two accurate units within a sentence. For example, the sequence between "the dog" would count as one CWS if both words were spelled and used correctly in the student's writing. The picture–word CBM-W prompt produces data that are as reliable and valid as standardized norm-referenced measures of writing (McMaster et al., 2011), with the added benefit that the assessment is closely related to typical curricular tasks.

The procedures for CBA-ID in writing use a curricular task such as the picture–word CBM-W prompt to produce instructionally relevant data. The first step is to administer the CBM-W prompt following the standardized administration guidelines (McMaster, Du, & Petursdottir, 2009). The second step is to score the student's performance on the CBM-W prompt using a defensible and useful metric such as CWS. Sample scoring rules for the CWS metric are included in Table 6.1. Following standardized administration and scoring rules ensures that the CBM-W data are as accurate and trustworthy as possible. The

TABLE 6.1. Sample Scoring Procedures for a Picture–Word Prompt

Materials

1. Colored pencils.
2. Scoring sheet and student packet.

Before scoring

1. Read the prompt and entire writing sample before scoring.
2. Do your best to decipher what the student is writing. Sounding out what your student wrote may help in deciphering a word.
3. Ignore spacing problems unless the sample is very difficult to read (i.e., if you can distinguish between words even though they are close together, count them as individual words).

Scoring procedures

1. Read the prompt and the entire writing sample.
2. Place a blue caret on both sides of correct word sequences.

Correct word sequence (CWS)

1. If two words in a row are spelled and used correctly, place a *blue* caret *above and between* the two words indicating a correct word sequence.
   Example: ^Tom^likes^ to^ play $_v$ bsbal $_v$. |^He ^hit^a^fast^ pitch $_v$ compleetly $_v$ over ^the $_v$fens$_v$. |
2. At the beginning of the sentence the word sequence is correct if
   a. The word is correct.
   b. The sentence begins with a capital.
3. If the last word and punctuation are correct, this is a CWS and a blue caret may be placed on both sides of the word.
4. A sentence ending without punctuation or with an incorrect punctuation is not a CWS.

TABLE 6.2. Instructional-Level Criteria for Writing

Measure	Frustration	Instructional level	Independent
Picture–word			
Words written	0 to 10	11 to 18	19 or higher
Words spelled correctly	0 to 8	9 to 14	15 or higher
Correct word sequences	0 to 7	8 to 14	15 or higher
Sentence copying			
Words written	0 to 13	14 to 19	20 or higher
Words spelled correctly	0 to 10	11 to 16	17 or higher
Correct word sequences	0 to 19	10 to 16	17 or higher

Note. Numbers are all totals from a 3 minute writing sample. Based on Parker, McMaster, and Burns (2011).

third step is to compare the resulting score with a set of empirically derived criteria for the instructional level, which are based on Parker and colleagues (2011) and are included in Table 6.2. Based on the student's score relative to the instructional-level criteria (i.e., above, within, below the instructional level), an appropriate instructional strategy can be identified (see Table 6.3 for a sample set of instructional strategies to be employed based on CBA-ID data). Finally, the strategy is implemented, and progress is monitored to ensure effectiveness (Parker, Burns, et al., 2012).

TABLE 6.3. Instructional Hierarchy Interventions for Writing Based on CBA-ID

CBA-ID level	Learning hierarchy stage	Instructional hierarchy	Interventions for writing
Frustration	Acquisition	Accuracy	• Explicit instruction in high-frequency spelling patterns • Explicit instruction in letter formation • Modeling intervention • Immediate feedback on accuracy
Instructional	Fluency	Proficiency	• Repeated practice intervention to improve automaticity • Incentives to produce more writing • Task choice • Delayed feedback
Independent	Generalization/ maintenance	Application across contexts	• Intervention using self-regulated strategy development
Independent	Adaptation	Application to solve problems	• Writing-to-learn interventions (Bangert-Drowns, Hurley, & Wilkenson, 2004)

TARGETING INTERVENTIONS USING CBA-ID DATA

The benefit of CBA-ID is that it helps take some of the guesswork out of identifying what type of intervention a struggling student needs. Imagine a typical first-grade classroom. It is not uncommon for several of those students to experience serious struggles with the classroom writing expectations. Any three students might refuse to write, write very little, or produce writing that is of such poor quality that it cannot be deciphered. Yet, despite the apparent similarity in their writing problems, a seasoned teacher knows that the same intervention approach will not work with each student. That teacher has likely experienced the frustration of an intervention working well with one student but not working with another. CBA-ID data provide guidance for selecting among different intervention procedures.

> **The benefit of CBA-ID is that it helps take some of the guesswork out of identifying what type of intervention a struggling student needs.**

As discussed in Chapter 2, CBA-ID data are used to understand skill development along a learning hierarchy, which in turn informs the instructional hierarchy (IH; Haring & Eaton, 1978). Each of the component writing skills (i.e., letter formation, spelling, sentence writing) follows that hierarchy. Students first learn how to perform each skill accurately. Next, they learn how to perform it proficiently and automatically. More proficient performance facilitates use of the skill in various contexts and for various activities (generalization). Finally, they learn to adapt and apply their writing skills for solving problems. Students who score within the frustration range are still learning how to perform the skill accurately, and those in the instructional-level range are ready to become more proficient in it. Once a student scores within the independent range, then he or she is ready to apply the skill to solve problems.

The skill of letter formation provides a clear illustration of the learning hierarchy. When young students first learn how to write a letter, they often make any number of errors. Think of the number of times a kindergartner reverses the formation of *b*s and *d*s, or how often students inaccurately make a *t* instead of an *f*. However, once they make the letter accurately, there is still a period of time in which they need to be very careful to do so. At this stage, the student writes his or her letters slowly and deliberately, or erases and rewrites the letter multiple times until it is right. The student knows how to write the letter accurately, just not automatically. Over time and repeated practice opportunities, the student can write the letter more proficiently. He or she then becomes much more successful at writing it in different contexts, such as on different worksheets or on the chalkboard or when asked by a parent to write it at home. Finally, the student who has mastered letter formation can use his or herskill in writing the letter to form basic words (e.g., *c* in *cat* or for a functional purpose such as *C* for *Claire* on a self-made greeting card).

Teaching practices and standards reflect an intuitive, if not intentional, understanding of this skill progression. Preschool and kindergarten classrooms are full of visual examples of letters, and teachers often use manipulatives, modeling, or letter–arrow diagrams to instruct students in accurately making letters. Most early elementary classrooms offer students ample opportunity to practice their writing skills to a proficient level (e.g., writer's workshop). In later elementary and beyond, teachers often provide exposure to various expository and narrative samples, graphic organizers, and other strategies to help students generalize and adapt their writing skills. For many students teaching strategies result in effective writing skills by middle-to-late elementary school. Unfortunately, a large portion of students' writing skills fail to flourish even when these instructional strategies are used. Struggling students need a more systematic approach to writing intervention that continues to capitalize on knowledge of how these skills develop. Below we discuss how CBA-ID data guide that decision making.

Frustration Level

Imagine one of the three students above is assessed using CBA-ID and the data show the student wrote two CWS within the 3-minute writing sample. That means the student produced two sequences of correctly spelled and used words within 3 minutes of writing, which falls within the frustration range according to Table 6.2. Asking him to write a paragraph on his recent trip to the zoo would likely result in considerable resistance. Asking him to practice his writing skills by journaling would probably result in lots of off-task behavior. His responses to these tasks simply serve to validate what the CBA-ID data found: His skills are within a frustration level for writing.

So what type of intervention does a student at the frustration level need? According to the IH (Haring & Eaton, 1978), this student needs modeling, explicit instruction, and immediate corrective feedback. It may be that the student struggles to spell high-frequency and basic sight words. If that is the primary problem, explicit instruction in letter–sound correspondence and common spelling patterns would be beneficial. Berninger and colleagues (1998) implemented a spelling intervention that explicitly taught and modeled common spelling patterns to students at risk of poor spelling outcomes, and results showed clear improvements for the students' spelling skills. Several tested strategies, all of which included explicitly teaching spelling skills, were effective in improving spelling skills. Intriguingly, students' compositional writing skills also improved, suggesting that the better spelling skills facilitated students' general writing development.

It may also be that the student struggles to accurately form the letters and words necessary for accurate writing. In a different study, Berninger and colleagues (1997) targeted a handwriting intervention to students at risk for poor handwriting outcomes, and similar to the spelling intervention, the handwriting intervention improved students' letter formation and overall writing compositional skills. Several intervention approaches that used explicit instruction and modeling resulted in increased handwriting, and some generalized to also increase compositional skills.

The results of interventions like those implemented by Berninger and colleagues (1997) show the benefits of providing students explicit instruction and modeling. However, the researchers made sure to target their interventions for students who exhibited the worst spelling and handwriting skills. Imagine if they had targeted these interventions to students who already had accurate spelling and handwriting skills. The students would have had to endure unnecessary instruction, with the results similar to those produced by Gickling and Armstrong (1978): the students might have maintained accurate responding—but that is likely because they already were accurate—and they could have shown much lower levels of on-task behavior.

Instructional Level

Imagine another of the three students above is assessed using CBA-ID and the data show the student wrote 12 CWS within the 3-minute writing sample. That means the student wrote 12 correctly spelled and used words within 3 minutes of writing, which according to Table 6.2 falls within the instructional-level range and suggests sufficient writing skills to spell and use words accurately when creating written text. For this student, additional explicit instruction and modeling is likely unnecessary. A good example for adults could be learning how to play golf: If after taking several golf lessons you could successfully hit the ball where you were aiming, would you keep going only to the driving range, or would you start going out on the course to practice? You would start going to the course to practice. A student who is in the instructional level for writing needs a similar approach to intervention designed to further improve writing skills.

In a study involving three first-grade students who exhibited very poor writing skills, Parker, Dickey, Burns, and McMaster (2012) worked with students whose initial CBA-ID data showed their writing skills were within, or very near, the instructional level. A different assessment procedure was used to target the actual interventions, but the results corresponded closely with what would be expected from CBA-ID procedures. Even though modeling conditions were tested, they did not improve student writing performance. One student benefited from an intervention that incorporated self-selection, which supports our interpretation of the expectancy–value theory discussed in Chapter 2: this student had sufficient skill in writing that, provided the task was not too challenging (i.e., his or her expectancy was not frustrating), he or she could benefit from an intervention that incorporated greater value in the task. The other two students benefited from interventions that included repeated writing and incentives for performance, which are both recommended approaches for students acquiring greater proficiency in academic skills (Haring & Eaton, 1978).

At this point it may be important to remember that even though CBA-ID results potentially show some students are at a frustration level, while others are at the instructional or independent levels, students can be struggling (or "frustrating") with writing regardless of what their CBA-ID data show. Two students may be showing similar topographies of struggling writing behavior, such as refusing to write, writing very little, or creating extremely poor text, but the same intervention may not work with both. CBA-ID helps successfully target interventions in an individualized way, and just because one student has CBA-ID data within the frustration level and another has data within the instructional level, it does not mean the one with higher data is struggling less than the one with lower data. Both are struggling, but their current skill level requires different intervention approaches.

Independent Level

This brings us to the third of the three struggling students. After being assessed with CBA-ID, the data showed the student wrote 28 CWS within the 3-minute writing sample. The student wrote almost 30 correctly spelled and used words within a short sample, and clearly has very accurate and proficient writing skills. Understandably, classroom instruction that includes heavy doses of explicit instruction, modeling, and practice are likely boring to this student. These data shed some light on why the student always seems to wander around the classroom bothering other students while they engage in independent writing. The data are also contradictory to the fact the student has not written even moderate quantities during the last several months of writing practice.

Aside from boredom, the most common problem facing students at an independent level is the use of their writing skills to write for a variety of purposes. Although fluent writers, they may fail to generalize their skills when writing expository stories, or they may fail to use their writing skills to complete a note sheet with observations during art class. In early elementary school, these needs may go unnoticed, but if their skills remain undeveloped, they become a greater problem as schooling progresses. A robust amount of research demonstrates that self-regulation strategies can be used to teach these struggling writers skills to organize, plan, apply, and monitor their writing.

As summarized by Graham and Perin (2007), self-regulated strategy development (SRSD; Harris & Graham, 1996) explicitly teaches students strategies using six stages of instruction:

1. Explicit instruction in background knowledge for using a specific writing strategy.
2. Description and discussion of the strategy.
3. Modeling of the strategy by the teacher.
4. Student memorization of the strategy (mnemonic strategies are often used).
5. Teacher support and scaffolding of the strategy as students start using it.
6. Student use of the strategy with little or no adult support.

Several studies have examined the use of SRSD, and results indicate it has strong and high-quality support (Baker, Chard, Ketterlin-Geller, Apichatabutra, & Doabler, 2009). For example, Lane and colleagues (2008) taught at-risk second graders with behavioral disorders how to plan their writing using a mnemonic called POW (Pick an idea, Organize the notes, and Write and say more) and using graphic organizers. They were then taught how to monitor their work with self-monitoring strategies that reminded students to check for main elements of their writing (e.g., who, what, when, where, how). All of the participating students made gains on important writing variables, including story completeness, length, and quality. Moreover, those gains were maintained 6 weeks later.

CONCLUSION

Students who have proficient writing skills can spell and use words effectively, but writing is a complex process and they may still require intervention support to be successful writers. SRSD is an example of an intervention that aligns with the IH stages of generalization and adaption (Haring & Eaton, 1978) that can be used to support students who are struggling to use writing across contexts and assignments. The application of SRSD further illustrates how CBA-ID data serve to effectively target research-based interventions to the students who need them. Just as a student at the independent level would not benefit from explicit instruction and modeling of spelling and handwriting skills even though interventions to build those skills are highly effective, a student who needs to improve accurate spelling and handwriting skills likely would not benefit from SRSD, even though it is a robust intervention. Fortunately, CBA-ID for writing results in reliable data that can be used to benefit intervention and instruction. Although more research is certainly needed, practitioners can confidently design instruction and intervention for writing with CBA-ID.

CHAPTER 7

CBA-ID for Instruction and Intervention

Our initial conceptualization of this book had two separate chapters for instruction and intervention, but we realized that was a mistake. We both consult with schools all over the country regarding response to intervention (RTI) and train school personnel on several aspects of an effective model including the role of CBA-ID. One common difficulty that we see is that for many schools, their first step in initiating their RTI model is to start a problem-solving team. In our opinion, and experience, that is a mistake for two important reasons.

The first reason why it is a mistake to initiate an RTI model by starting a problem-solving team is that effective problem solving is an intense process. It generally requires five to eight professionals meeting for 15 to 30 minutes to discuss one student. Effective problem solving also involves in-depth problem analysis to determine appropriate interventions. We have written about this process in more depth elsewhere (Burns, Riley-Tillman, & VanDerHeyden, 2012) and will not go into detail here, but will consider the implications of using a problem-solving team as the first step in an RTI model based on a typical school. If a school has 450 students, and on average 20% of the students need additional support beyond quality core instruction, then 90 students in the elementary school would need to be discussed by the problem-solving team. Imagine trying to schedule a problem-solving team meeting for 90 students. If the team meets once each week and discusses two students each time, that is 45 weeks, which exceeds the length of the school year for most schools. Most schools just do not have the resources needed to conduct a problem-solving team meeting for 90 students; the system will crumble under its own weight. Schools first need a Tier 2 intervention that focuses on approximately 15% of the students and targets the intervention with low-level analysis. Having a strong Tier 2 will get that number from 90 down to 25 or 30, which is a much more reasonable number. Thus, without an effective Tier 2, you cannot have an effective problem-solving team process (Tier 3).

The second reason why starting a problem-solving team is not an effective way to begin an RTI initiative is that it ignores an important issue. Many of the schools in which we work have more than 20% of the students who need additional support. Consider a classroom of 25 students in which 15 of them are identified as needing intervention. Could the school personnel really pull 15 of 25 students to run a small-group intervention? No, they could not. In this far too common example, there is a system issue and that system issue must be addressed before starting interventions. There appears to be a potential misalignment between the core instruction and the needs of a majority of the students. We are not saying that core instruction is of poor quality, although it might be. We are saying that at the very least, the current core instruction is not improving the learning of these 25 students and needs to be changed. Thus, an RTI model should begin by focusing on core instruction. Without a quality Tier 2, there cannot be an effective Tier 3, and even before that, without an effective Tier 1 (core instruction), there cannot be an effective Tier 2. Without good core instruction, nothing else matters! The importance of quality core instruction is often missed when RTI initiatives begin by starting a problem-solving team.

The comments above are not intended to be critical of RTI. However, school personnel should conceptualize RTI differently than we have before. RTI came out of special education legislation that stated when identifying a child with a learning disability, a local educational agency may "use a process based on the child's response to scientific, research-based intervention" (34 C.F.R. § 300.307[a][2]). RTI is the process of providing quality instruction and intervention, and using student learning in response to that instruction to make instructional and important educational decisions (Batsche et al., 2005). The focus of an RTI model is on measuring student response to instruction and intervention. However, many states are adopting the term multi-tiered system of support (MTSS) because it focuses on providing instruction and intervention. RTI came out of special education law, but MTSS focuses on general education. RTI is assessment oriented, but MTSS emphasizes providing services. Both rely on screening all students, providing tiered interventions, and monitoring student progress, but MTSS has a more explicit focus on general education.

We prefer the term MTSS over RTI. As discussed above, many RTI models rely heavily on problem-solving teams, which we pointed out as problematic. MTSS models are driven by effective grade-level teams functioning as professional learning communities (PLCs), which examine student outcome data within a culture of collaboration to enhance student learning (DuFour, 2005). PLCs can examine core instructional issues, but problem-solving teams generally do not. Moreover, PLCs are responsible for examining student data within an MTSS to determine who needs Tier 2 or Tier 3 intervention, what type of intervention a student needs, and if the student is making sufficient progress. Therefore, classroom teachers are more closely involved in designing interventions within MTSS, which results in the direct link between instruction and intervention that has often been missing in previous intervention models.

Because classroom teachers are more closely involved in intervention decisions within the MTSS model, it did not make sense to provide information in two separate chapters. The purpose of this book is to explain how the evidence-based practices that derive from CBA-ID research can be applied across the tiers of the MTSS model. To illustrate, Table 7.1

TABLE 7.1. Sample Interventions Targeted using CBA-ID

Reading	Math	Written expression
	Tier 1	
Partner reading to build fluency or peer tutoring for basic reading skills	Peer tutoring for fact fluency skills	Peer tutoring for spelling skills to support writing
	Tier 2	
Homogeneous skill grouping to target phonics skills	Small-group fact fluency intervention aligned with core sequence	Intervention targeting accurate handwriting skills
	Tier 3	
Incremental rehearsal to target key vocabulary words	Explicit instruction in math concepts	Explicit modeling intervention for sentence writing

displays interventions that could be targeted at all three tiers. Below we discuss in more detail how to use CBA-ID in core instruction, and in designing Tier 2 and Tier 3 interventions.

USING CBA-ID IN TIER 1: SUPPORTING CORE INSTRUCTION

Reading instruction has changed dramatically in the past 10 years. The National Reading Panel (2000) report refocused reading instruction on decoding and emphasized the importance of phonemic awareness. The proverbial pendulum had swung far toward literacy-based instruction that emphasized context and meaning before the National Reading Panel changed the conversation. The pendulum has currently settled more in the middle between code-based and meaning-based instruction with the current movement toward balanced instruction (Pressley, 2006), in which guided reading is an essential component.

Guided reading is an instructional approach that involves grouping students who are at similar points in their development in order to address individual needs of students while teaching them to (1) read increasingly difficult texts with understanding and fluency; (2) to construct meaning, and (3) strategies to read words with which they are unfamiliar (Iaqunita, 2006). Unfortunately, guided reading has become synonymous with leveled reading in which teachers simply group students according to a score on an informal reading inventory such as the Fountas and Pinnell Benchmark Assessment System (F&P; Fountas & Pinnell, 2007). We discussed the considerable shortcomings of the F&P assessment in Chapter 3, but even classroom teachers who might be skeptical about the practical considerations for psychometrics would probably agree that one score (e.g., reading level M) cannot capture the entire universe of reading skills and materials. Thus, we frequently see students grouped together who do not have similar skills or reading levels.

CBA-ID would allow for much more flexible grouping. The F&P is only administered two, three, or four times each year, but CBA-ID could be conducted as frequently as the teacher needed. More frequent assessments would be advantageous because educators know through experience that reading is a dynamic skill that can rapidly change. Moreover, CBA-ID can be used to assess subskills, as described below, to determine the appropriate instructional target. Ironically, Fountas and Pinnell's (1996) initial description of guided reading emphasized that some students may be working on basic reading skills while some students work on more advanced skills and complex text. CBA-ID provides data that can be used to determine which students need basic skills and which need more complex text.

There are several ways to determine instructional levels in the classroom. The teacher could begin by assessing every student at the beginning of the year with grade-level text, which would only require 1–3 minutes per student. If a CBA-ID of contextual reading identifies students who read less than 93% correct, they could be assessed with a CBA-ID that focused on decoding (Chapter 4). If a student did not correctly complete at least 85% of the items on the decoding-focused CBA-ID, then he or she should focus on basic decoding skills during guided reading. Students who correctly completed more than 90% of the decoding tasks could be assessed using survey-level CBA-ID of contextual reading to find material that represented appropriately challenging text at a level that is easier than the given grade, and they would be grouped together to have some combination of basic skill building with reading simple text. Students who read between 93 and 97% on grade-level text could be grouped together, and those who read above 97% could be assessed with continuously more difficult text to determine their skill level.

Assume that there are 25 students in the classroom and eight of them read between 93 and 97% correct on grade-level material. We are simulating these numbers, but are doing so from our experience. If there were eight students whose instructional level was consistent with the grade level, then they would only require about 25 total minutes to assess. If there are nine students for whom the grade-level text represented the frustration level (i.e., less than 93% correct), then they would require a decoding assessment and perhaps additional connected text assessments, which would likely require 3 additional minutes per student or 27 minutes, for a total of 50–55 minutes. Finally, additional assessments would be needed for the 8 remaining students who read more than 97% correct on grade-level text. If we required three additional assessments to find their instructional level, then that would result in an additional 24 minutes for a total of 50–55 minutes as well. Therefore, the entire process would require approximately 1.5 to 2.0 hours, which is considerably less time than most informal reading inventories (IRIs) that require 15–30 minutes per student. Indeed, if those 25 students took only 15 minutes per IRI assessment, the total amount of assessment time would be over 6 hours!

Teachers could conduct CBA-ID to determine guided reading groups every month, but also on a more frequent basis with individual children who seem to be making strong progress or lacking in growth. In between the assessments, teachers could also conduct a 1-minute CBA-ID with each student using grade-level text on a weekly basis, or some classroom teachers with whom we have worked taught their students to read into a recorder, which can then be scored later and be used to give the students feedback.

Classwide Needs

It would go beyond the scope of this chapter to discuss what constitutes quality instruction in reading and math, but previous research by VanDerHeyden and colleagues has highlighted the prevalence and importance of identifying classwide problems (VanDerHeyden & Burns, 2005b; VanDerHeyden, Witt, & Gilbertson, 2007; VanDerHeyden, Witt, & Naquin, 2003). If a classwide problem exists, then it may be more efficient to bring the intervention to the class than it would be to pull students out for interventions at the selected level (Tier 2). Thus, the first step to implementing an MTSS is to identify or rule out classwide problems.

A classwide need is identified by computing the class median and comparing that median to a national standard. We suggest using the 25th percentile or perhaps the 40th percentile. We tend to favor the 25th percentile, but local policy can vary from that depending on the needs of the students and the characteristics of the schools (e.g., more affluent schools may want to use the 40th or even 50th percentile). Median is used because averages can be disproportionally affected by outlying data for small data sets (e.g., less than 30 data points), and the median is not susceptible to outliers.

Finding the class median is quite easy in most data management systems, and can be done in Microsoft Excel by simply selecting the MEDIAN function from the function wizard. Brief directions are also listed in Table 7.2. The median score for the first set of data would be 100, and it would be 89 for the second set. Those two scores fell at the 50th and

TABLE 7.2. Finding the Median Percentile Rank

Example 1 raw scores			Example 1 sorted scores			Example 2 raw scores			Example 2 sorted scores		
Student	Score	%ile	Student	Score	%ile	Student	Score	%ile	Student	Score	%ile
A	100	50	B	125	95	A	73	4	J	130	98
B	125	95	I	117	87	B	89	23	E	101	53
C	90	25	J	110	75	C	82	12	D	98	45
D	70	2	K	106	66	D	98	45	G	90	25
E	80	9	A	100	50	E	101	53	B	89	23
F	98	45	G	100	50	F	85	16	F	85	16
G	100	50	F	98	45	G	90	25	C	82	12
H	89	23	C	90	25	H	76	5	I	80	9
I	117	87	H	89	23	I	80	9	H	76	5
J	110	75	E	80	9	J	130	98	A	73	4
K	106	66	D	70	2						

1. Reorder data from highest to lowest.
2. With an odd number of data points (11), the median is the middle score—5 above and 5 below.
3. The median is Student F with a score of 100, 50th percentile.

1. Reorder data from highest to lowest.
2. With an even number of data points (10), the median is the average of two middle scores (Students B and F).
3. The median is the average of 89 (Student B) and 85 (Student F), which is 87, 19th percentile.

19th percentile rank, respectively, based on a national sample. It is important to compare class medians with a national sample so as not to be skewed by local circumstances. The first set of data in Table 7.2 does not indicate any difficulties because the score is at the 50th percentile. The median score for the second set of data fell below the 25th percentile and suggests a classwide need.

Procedures to Identify and Remediate Classwide Problems

Reading

Curriculum-based measures (CBMs; Deno, 1985) are often selected for screening because they are quick (most are administered in 1 minute), have well-established psychometrically sound properties (Marston, 1989; Wayman et al., 2007), are predictive of later reading skills (McGlinchey & Hixson, 2004; Stage & Jacobsen, 2001), and align with classroom instruction in most cases (Powell-Smith & Bradley-Klug, 2001). Oral reading fluency (ORF) is the measure most often used to screen for grades 1 through 5, and ORF data correlate highly with performance on statewide achievement tests ($r = .69$; Yeo, 2009).

ORF assessments consist of asking students to read from a grade-level passage for 1 minute. Thus, CBM-ORF assessments tend to closely resemble CBA-ID on the surface. Much like CBA-ID, hesitations of longer than 2 seconds, omissions, and substitutions are counted as errors when conducting CBM-ORF assessments. The final score is the number of words read correctly. Three 1-minute administrations are generally given for screening assessments, and the median number of words read correctly per minute (WCPM) is recorded as the ORF score.

As noted previously, we typically identify classwide needs by comparing the median ORF score with the 25th percentile. For example, the 25th percentile for ORF in the fall of fourth grade is 81 WCPM (Aimsweb, 2010), and a median score equal to or less than 81 would suggest a classwide need. We often implement an intervention protocol based on Fuchs, Fuchs, Mathes, and Simmons (1997) that can be downloaded for free at *www.cehd. umn.edu/reading/PRESS/resources/interventions.html*, but some teachers may want to target their intervention efforts more precisely, which is where CBA-ID comes in.

After classwide need is identified, teachers can use CBA-ID practices to then convert the score to a percentage by dividing the number of WCPM from the ORF assessment by the total number of words (number of WCPM plus number of errors). If the score falls below 93%, then the teacher has two options depending on the age of the students. With older students in third or fourth grades and higher, the teacher could conduct a series of CBA-ID with the students to determine books in which the students can read 93–97% of the words correct (i.e., their instructional level). The teacher may also be able to just use typed one-page probes that are available for free online to make the process easier. Then, students would be allowed to practice reading from those passages for 15 minutes each day to build fluency. With first- through third-grade students, a median score of less than 93% correct could suggest that they are struggling to apply code-based skills, and additional classwide remediation/reteaching of decoding skills may be more appropriate.

We suggest taking no more than 15–20 minutes each day for the classwide intervention and monitoring progress for all students at least twice each month, preferably once each week. Once the class median exceeds the 25th percentile on two consecutive assessments, then the classwide intervention can stop.

Math

Math skills are directly linked to the quality of instruction (Fuchs, Fuchs, & Karns, 2001). Many schools screen the math skills of all students three times each year with curriculum-based measurement for math (CBM-M). However, the link between CBM-M and instruction is not often clear (Shapiro, 2012) and other measures predicted state test scores among third- and fourth-grade students better than CBM-M (Shapiro & Gebhardt, 2012). Finally, the criteria for CBM-M are not as well defined as they are for reading. Thus, schools are frequently using group-administered math assessments such as Measures of Academic Progress (Northwest Evaluation Association, 2003) and Star Math (Renaissance Learning, 2011). One advantage of group-administered commercially prepared assessments is that they are efficient with psychometrically sound data because groups of students can complete the tests in a matter of 15–30 minutes and can instantaneously score and report the results.

We suggest that schools can screen with CBM-M or some group-administered math measure, but that they also develop a series of single-skill measures based on their objectives (see Chapter 5) and conduct a series of CBA-ID as well. Once the screening data are collected and a classwide need is identified (i.e., the median score falls at or below the 25th percentile), then CBA-ID is conducted with specific objectives to determine where to start interventions. For example, consider the potential sequence of skills outlined in Table 7.3, which is based on research by VanDerHeyden and Burns (2009) to determine a meaningful sequence of math objectives. The classroom teacher would have his or her students com-

TABLE 7.3. Sample Math Objectives for Second and Third Grades

Second grade	Third grade
1. Addition facts 0–20	1. Addition and subtraction facts 0–20
2. Subtraction facts 0–9	2. Fact families addition and subtraction 0–20
3. Subtraction facts 0–12	3. Three-digit addition
4. Subtraction facts 0–15	4. Three-digit subtraction
5. Subtraction facts 0–20	5. Two- and three-digit addition and subtraction
6. Mixed subtraction/addition 0–20	6. Multiplication facts 0–9
7. Two-digit addition without regrouping	7. Division facts 0–9
8. Two-digit addition with regrouping	8. Add and subtract fractions with like denominators
9. Two-digit subtraction without regrouping	9. Single digit multiplied by double/triple digits
10. Two-digit subtraction with regrouping	10. Single digit divided into double/triple digits without remainders
11. Three-digit addition	11. Add and subtract decimals to the hundredths
12. Three-digit subtraction	

Note. Based on VanDerHeyden and Burns (2009).

plete single-skill CBA-ID probes for each objective and score them with digits correct per minute (DCPM; see Chapter 5). The data would then be compared with the instructional-level criteria of 14–31 DCPM for second and third grades, and 24–49 DCPM for fourth and fifth grades.

If the classwide need was identified in the fall, then assessments would start with the first objective and would progress forward in the sequence. For example, with second graders, they would be given a probe that contained addition facts from 0 to 20. If the median number of DCPM for the class fell above 31, then the students would be administered a probe that contained subtraction facts 0–9, and so on until the median score fell within the instructional-level range. The teacher could then begin intervention at that point in the objectives. If the classwide need was identified with spring data, then the teacher could begin with the final objective and progress backward until an instructional level was found. Classwide needs detected in January would result in starting with the middle objective (e.g., mixed subtraction/addition 0–20) and working forward if the score fell within the independent range or backward if it fell in the frustration range.

Classwide intervention can be considered supplemental instruction, but cannot replace core instruction. Intervention protocols used by VanDerHeyden utilize peer tutoring to deliver fact-fluency interventions, which is likely appropriate for most instances at the elementary level because most math difficulties with students this age are linked to an inability to recall the facts fast enough to apply them (Geary et al., 2007; Hanich et al., 2001), and fact-based remediation has been shown to be effective in improving student achievement (Burns, Kanive, & DeGrande, 2012; Codding, Chan-Iannetta, Palmer, & Lukito, 2009; Van-DerHeyden & Burns, 2005b).

Classwide interventions generally require approximately 10–15 minutes per day and involve having students pair up in a heterogeneous dyad, practice single-skill computation for 2 minutes with worksheets for flash cards, score each other's work, and provide them feedback on the accuracy of their work (VanDerHeyden & Burns, 2005b). Students are then assessed each week and the intervention continues until the class median exceeds the instructional-level range, at which time the class moves to the next core objective.

Writing

Effective core instruction for writing includes assignment of varied writing tasks along with support to complete them, explicit modeling of writing skills and processes, and regular follow-up and feedback by the teacher to improve writing skills (Graham et al., 2001). In practice, these instructional activities are implemented in widely varying degrees (Cutler & Graham, 2008), but research acknowledges the importance of explicit and research-based practices for at-risk students (Graham & Harris, 1994). A systematic approach to targeting core writing activities could be informed by implementing CBA-ID procedures at the class level.

Unlike reading and math, routine classwide assessment practices for writing appear to be much less common. However, CBM approaches for writing are available across various grades, from kindergarten (Coker & Ritchey, 2010) and early elementary (McMaster et al., 2011) through secondary levels (McMaster & Espin, 2007). Screening data from these assessments could help educators target which skills to teach and how to teach them. Additional research is necessary across all ages of writing development, but the CBA-ID procedures described in Chapter 6 hold strong promise for remediating and preventing classwide issues in early writing (Graham et al., 2001).

Procedures in early writing could start by administering a CBM for writing, such as the picture–word prompt (McMaster et al., 2009). Student performance would then be scored on a metric that produces data to indicate skill level on developmentally important transcription skills (Berninger & Amtmann, 2003). For example, the CWS metric provides information on student spelling, handwriting, and basic syntax skills. As such, classwide medians on the CWS metric are broadly indicative of students' overall skills in those areas. If the classwide median is around 5 CWS, for example, that means the students produced little accurate text in 3 minutes of writing, indicating most students struggle with accurately producing even basic writing skills. This class would benefit from additional instructional focus on the accurate transcription skills like handwriting and spelling (Graham et al., 2001). If, however, the classwide median is around 25 CWS, that means the students are already producing text accurately and relatively proficiently; additional instruction in basic writing skills such as handwriting and simple spelling is likely unnecessary. This class would likely benefit from additional instructional focus on using strategy-based processes to write more complex texts (e.g., Harris & Graham, 1996).

Similar instructional benefits exist for repeatedly using CBA-ID in writing as in reading and math. CBA-ID data can be collected after focusing instruction on the needs of the class to provide ongoing assessment data support decisions to change or maintain the instructional focus. For a class whose median CWS score in the fall is 5, effective classwide instruction of basic transcription skills using peer strategies (e.g., Maheady, Harper, Mallette, & Winstanley, 1991) might result in a subsequent median score of 12 CWS in late November of the school year. At that time, the classwide CBA-ID data that indicate instruction to help students produce accurate basic transcription skills may no longer be necessary; however, the students continue to need classwide instruction to proficiently produce basic transcription skills.

USING CBA-ID IN TIER 2: TARGETING SMALL-GROUP INTERVENTIONS

Once classwide needs are remediated or ruled out, then school personnel can target supplemental intervention to individual students who continue to need support. Many schools administer multiple screening measures including CBM for reading and math, and a group-administered measure of comprehension (e.g., MAP-R) for reading or of applications for math (e.g., MAP-M). These two sources of data together provide a solid picture of a student's overall proficiency, but the accuracy with which students read can also provide useful information. Students who read less than 93% of the words correctly are likely struggling to decode the text and would likely benefit from reading intervention. Other reading skills that do not involve reading connected text (e.g., letter–sound fluency or math facts) should be completed with 90% accuracy (Burns, 2004b). Thus, students who score below the 25th percentile (or 40th) and who correctly read less than 93% of the words in reading assessments or 90% of the items from other assessments, would be identified as needing additional support.

Tier 2 interventions are usually implemented in small groups. Research syntheses support homogeneous groupings for specific subjects including reading (Slavin, 1987), and instruction that is geared toward areas for preventative intervention increases student learning (Connor, Morrison, Fishman, Schatschneider, & Underwood, 2007). Below we discuss how to use CBA-ID to determine the intervention targets for students who need a supplemental support.

Procedures to Determine Intervention Targets

Reading

Once students are identified as needing supplemental interventions, teams then can turn their attention to creating small groups and identifying areas for preventative intervention. Given their supplemental nature, Tier 2 interventions generally target the same skills that are targeted in Tier 1 instruction and should also be aligned with the benchmarking measures used for that grade. Additionally, Tier 2 interventions should target critical basic reading skills, such as those identified by the National Reading Panel (2000): phonemic awareness, phonics, reading fluency, comprehension, and vocabulary.

The areas of reading instruction identified by the National Reading Panel provide a useful heuristic to target reading interventions (Burns, Christ, Boice, & Szadokierski, 2010). Students generally progress from phonemic awareness to alphabetic principles and decoding to reading fluently to comprehending what they read (Adams, 1990; Chall, 1983), but this sequence is even more relevant for struggling readers (Berninger et al., 2006; Snow et al., 1998). As mentioned above, struggling readers who read more than 93% of words correctly and who demonstrate sufficient reading fluency would likely benefit from interventions that target reading comprehension. However, children who read less than 93% might struggle with decoding or might need additional remediation with instructional-level reading fluency.

To further differentiate reading intervention targets, a series of assessments could be used to more precisely focus on the skill deficit. Teachers and interventionists could begin by conducting a decoding assessment. Nonsense-word fluency (NWF) is an acceptable measure of decoding skills and may help with deciding which reading area to target intervention. We frequently hear teachers object to the use of NWF, with good reason. NWF is not a good measure of overall reading because there may be proficient readers who struggle with NWF. However, if we do not conceptualize it as a general outcome measure (GOM), but instead as a subskill mastery measure (SMM; see Chapter 3), then NWF can be useful. In other words, if teachers are looking for a measure of overall reading skills, then NWF should not be used, but if they want a measure of how well a student can decode words for which there is no way to read them other than decoding them, then NWF and other pseudoword measures can work quite well. Additionally, teachers may question the validity of NWF and other pseudoword approaches for English language learners, but research has consistently indicated that NWF measures result in valid decisions for students for whom English is not their primary language (Fein et al., 2008; Vanderwood, Linklater, & Healy, 2008).

NWF and other skills measured within reading do not fall under the umbrella of reading for comprehension. Therefore, the instructional level for NWF would be 85–90% correct rather than 93–97% correct. If a student scores low on a reading screener such as oral reading fluency, then he or she could be administered an NWF or other pseudoword measure, and a score of less than 90% correct would suggest a deficit in decoding skills. Word lists of highly decodable but low-frequency real words may also work, and would also use 85–90% correct as the criterion, but research is not as well established for that type of measure as it is for NWF. Students in second grade or lower who score below 85% correct on a decoding measure could be assessed for phonemic awareness with measures such as phoneme segmentation fluency (PSF), which would also use 85–90% correct as the criterion.

Teachers and school psychologists would essentially work backward in the developmental process to identify the intervention target as outlined in Table 7.4. Essentially, the grade-level team would be attempting to identify the most fundamental skill in which the student struggles and would start the intervention at that point. Students would then be grouped based on the intervention target (comprehension, fluency, decoding, or phonemic awareness) and a standardized intervention could be delivered to address that skill. For

TABLE 7.4. Targeting Reading Interventions with CBA-ID

Student data	Follow-up assessment	Intervention target
Scores below 25th or 40th percentile on comprehension measure.	Assess reading fluency • Reads 93%+ words correctly	Comprehension
Scores low on comprehension but reads less than 93% of words correctly.	Assess decoding skills (e.g., NWF) • Reads 90%+ of sounds correctly	Reading fluency
Student in grades 3 through 12 scores low on comprehension, low on fluency, and does not read at least 85% of NWF sounds correctly.		Reading decoding
Student in grades K through 2 scores low on comprehension, low on fluency, and does not read at least 85% of NWF sounds correctly.	Assess phonemic awareness (e.g., PSF) • Correctly segments at least 90% of words correctly • Does not correctly segment at least 90% of sounds correctly	Reading decoding Phonemic awareness

example, students who struggle with phonemic awareness could participate in Road to the Code (Blachman, Ball, Black, & Tangel, 2000), but students who struggle with phonics could use Phonics for Reading (Archer, Flood, Lapp, & Lungren, 2011) or REWARDS (Archer, Gleason, & Vachon, 2006) for decoding.

Math

Tier 2 math interventions within an RTI framework are based on objectives that can be used to identify intervention targets. Essentially, practitioners can conduct CBA-ID in specific math objectives, as in Table 7.2, to determine the appropriate starting point for intervention. As described above, teachers and school psychologists could conduct each objective and work backward or forward in the sequence until the instructional level is found (14–31 DCPM for second and third graders, and 24–49 DCPM for fourth- and fifth-grade students), and then the students would be grouped to receive an intervention.

There are many free websites available with which single-skill probes can be created including *www.mathfactcafe.com*, *www.aplusmath.com*, and *www.interventioncentral.com*, but the sequencing of the skills is important for CBA-ID. After creating the probes, the sequence of the skills within the curriculum will determine the sequence with which the probes are used. There is often not a research-based sequence to the skills within the curriculum, so practitioners should likely rely on the sequence in which they are actually taught in the local curriculum.

Once the objective to target is identified, school personnel could group the children and deliver an intervention to address that objective. There are fewer commercially prepared small-group interventions for math then there are for reading, but research has identified potential approaches. According to the National Mathematics Advisory Panel (2008), fluent computation is an important goal for math, which could provide the basis for small-group interventions because students who struggle in math often struggle to recall basic facts (Geary et al., 2007; Hanich et al., 2001). An inability to recall basic facts well enough to use them in practice could interfere with completing more advanced problems (Houchins, Shippen, & Flores, 2004).

Tier 2 interventions in math frequently address fluent computation of basic skills. In fact, practice with basic math facts has been used as a remediation tool with considerable success (Ysseldyke, Thill, Pohl, & Bolt, 2005), and has effectively served as a Tier 2 intervention for math (Burns et al., 2012). Previous research used practice of basic math facts with student dyads to provide an array of problem examples and extensive feedback (VanDer-Heyden & Burns, 2005b). There are several easy-to-use group math intervention protocols that are available for free at *www.gosbr.net/math* and were developed from research by Amanda VanDerHeyden. However, as is always the case, it is not the lack of a research-based intervention that leads to less-than-desired results, it is the mismatch between intervention

> **It is not the lack of a research-based intervention that leads to less-than-desired results, it is the mismatch between intervention and student deficit.**

and student deficit. CBA-ID of skills represented within the sequence of a curriculum's objectives could help better match intervention and student skill.

Writing

Tier 2 interventions for writing are similar in concept to those for reading and math. They are targeted and focused on skill objectives. Like reading and math, efficient targeting (i.e., minimal data analysis) and delivery (i.e., often in groups) are important considerations. Writing objectives should be informed by writing development, and CBA-ID data can be used to determine which objectives are appropriate targets for individual students based on the assessment results.

Several theories of writing development have been researched by writing experts, but the most common focus is on the writing performance of adults and the purposes behind composing written text (e.g., cognitive/motivational models; Hayes, 1996). They give little attention to the importance of lower-level, earlier-developing writing skills (Berninger et al., 1992), and these skills are more often the cause of writing problems for school-age children.

Berninger and her colleagues (e.g., Berninger et al., 1992, 2002; Graham, Berninger, Abbott, Abbott, & Whitaker, 1997) researched the importance of transcription skills to later writing skills. They interpreted their results in light of a "simple view of writing," which proposed that the process of writing could be conveyed graphically by the idea of a triangle (see Figure 7.1), of which the top vertex is text generation, which in turn rests on transcription and self-regulatory skills, represented by the bottom two vertices (see Berninger & Amtmann, 2003, for more information).

A key concept within the theory is that of limited working memory resources, which are drawn on more or less for different skills depending on the development of other skills. For example, when transcription skills are low, much more working memory is required to demonstrate them. Think of the student who knows how to make a *b* but writes and erases

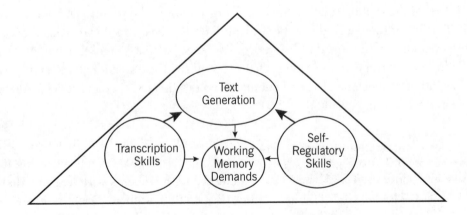

FIGURE 7.1. Simple view of writing development.

multiple attempts that included d and p; the skill of writing b is certainly present, but he or she is leveraging considerable working memory capacity toward remembering how it is written. This leaves less working memory for self-regulatory processes and text generation (McCutchen, 1996). Alternatively, the more automatic transcription skills become, the more cognitive resources are available for self-regulatory skills like planning and developing content. It is the importance ascribed to transcription skills that makes the simple view of writing development potentially useful for explaining writing development in school-age children, and CBA-ID data provide important information regarding students' current development of writing transcription skills.

As described in Chapter 6, CBA-ID data can be interpreted to determine the intervention approach that is best matched to the student's current skill. Students who are at a frustration level need intervention to build transcription skills, and may benefit from interventions targeting handwriting (Berninger et al., 1997) or spelling (Berninger et al., 1998). A subskill analysis of the student's writing sample used to collect the CBA-ID data can provide information to determine if spelling or handwriting skills are a better target for individual students, or alternatively, the CBA-ID writing sample can be scored for a metric that directly accounts for spelling skills (Parker et al., 2011). Students who are at an instructional level are those who have sufficiently accurate transcription skills, but may struggle with proficient demonstration of those skills. Intervention therefore seeks to improve the automaticity with which students can perform these skills. Finally, students at the independent level are those who can proficiently produce transcription skills, but they need additional intervention to develop self-regulatory skills (Harris & Graham, 1996) and apply their writing skills across contexts or to use in applied senses (e.g., to solve problems or facilitate learning in the content areas; Bangert-Drowns et al., 2004).

USING CBA-ID IN TIER 3: INFORMING INDIVIDUALIZED INTERVENTIONS

A strong Tier 2 intervention reduces the number of students who require an intensive intervention (Tier 3), but there will always be students whose needs are so severe that individualized interventions will be needed. Moreover, we suggest that school personnel consider special education a Tier 3 intervention. That is not to say that all students receiving Tier 3 are participating in special education, but all students who are receiving special education are receiving a Tier 3 intervention.

> **Strong Tier 2 interventions reduce the number of students requiring intensive interventions (Tier 3), but there will always be students with needs so severe that individualized interventions are required.**

CBA-ID was developed to help address the needs of students with the most severe difficulties and much of the research regarding it was conducted with students with learning disabilities (Burns, 2007; Burns, Dean, & Foley, 2004; Gickling & Armstrong, 1978). Therefore, the research and procedures developed from it have direct implications for students with significant difficulties regardless of whether they are identified with a disability or not. Below we discuss potential interventions based on CBA-ID research for students with significant learning difficulties.

Incremental Rehearsal

Incremental rehearsal (IR; Tucker, 1989) is a commonly used flash-card intervention that uses a high percentage of known items (e.g., one unknown item to eight or nine known) with high opportunities to respond. We discuss IR first because it is a generic intervention that can be applied to any academic task that requires students learn something that needs to be automatically recalled. The procedures for IR are outlined in Table 7.5. It is based on the principles of the instructional level because it includes a high percentage of known items (e.g., 83% with five known, 89% with eight known, and 90% with nine known), and because IR is often used as the intervention within CBA-ID research to provide intervention to students who perform a skill below 85–90% accurately. Previous research found that IR was effective in teaching words (Burns, 2007; Nist & Joseph, 2008; Szadokierski & Burns, 2008), math facts (Burns, 2005; Codding, Archer, & Connell, 2010), letter sounds (Burns & Kimosh, 2005; Volpe, Burns, DuBois, & Zaslofsky, 2011), and vocabulary (Burns, Dean, & Foley, 2004; Burns, Hodgson, Parker, & Fremont, 2011), among others.

The number of known items varies depending on the student. As stated in Table 7.5, children in preschool through first grade generally require five known items, but older children require more. We suggest starting with eight known items, but if the students seems bored, then it is too easy and known items can be removed, but do not go below five known items. If the student retains less than 90% of the information 1 day later, then add known items to generate additional repetition, but do not go above nine known items.

The procedures presented in Table 7.5 are generic, but apply to letter sounds, words, math facts, spelling, and so on. When teaching words, ask the student to use the unknown word in a sentence when it is first presented (Step 4). If the word is used grammatically and semantically correctly, even if the sentence is simplistic, then reinforce the child and move to Step 5. If the word is not correctly used, then provide a short definition or synonym, and use the word in a sentence. Next, ask the child to make up a different sentence with the word in it and move to the next step if he or she does so correctly. Math facts are straightforward in that the fact is presented (e.g., $4 \times 4 = ?$) and direct the student to say "four times four equals sixteen" each time it is presented. Spelling is conducted in a similar matter, except the words are written and starts somewhat differently. Known and unknowns are identified by asking the student to spell each word on a small portable whiteboard after you orally state the word. Words correctly spelled within 5 seconds are considered known. Next, write down the first unknown word on the whiteboard and orally read it to the student while pointing at the individual letters. Have the student copy the word by tracing it while saying the letters orally, then cover the word with your hand and ask the student to spell the word from memory. Remove your hand and have the student compare his or her spelling with the model. If it is correct, then say "Good job" and proceed to the next step. If the word is not

TABLE 7.5. Procedures for Implementing Incremental Rehearsal

1. Begin by assessing known and unknown items. Present the stimulus (e.g., words, letters, math facts) and ask the student to respond (e.g., state the words, state the letter sound, or state the answer to the math fact). Any correct response within 2 seconds is considered known, and those not correctly read within 2 seconds are unknown.

2. Write each unknown item on a $3'' \times 5''$ index card. Words and letters are generally written with a landscape orientation. Math facts should be written with the orientation (landscape or portrait) that is most often used to teach and test math facts within the curriculum.

3. Write five to nine items that the student can correctly respond within 1 second on index cards to serve as known items. Young children (e.g., kindergarten and first grade) usually need five known items, but older students require seven to nine known items.

4. Present the first unknown item to the student while verbally modeling the correct response. Next, ask the student to orally restate the correct response.

5. Rehearse the unknown item with the following sequence and ask the student to state the correct response every time it is presented:

   a. Present the first unknown item and the first known item.
   b. Present the first unknown item, the first known item, and the second known item.
   c. Present the first unknown item, the first known item, the second known item, and the third known item.
   d. Present the first unknown item, the first known item, the second known item, the third known item, and the fourth known item.
   e. Present the first unknown item, the first known item, the second known item, the third known item, the fourth known item, and the fifth known item.
   f. Present the first unknown item, the first known item, the second known item, the third known item, the fourth known item, the fifth known item, and the sixth known item.
   g. Present the first unknown item, the first known item, the second known item, the third known item, the fourth known item, the fifth known item, the sixth known item, and the seventh known item.
   h. Present the first unknown item, the first known item, the second known item, the third known item, the fourth known item, the fifth known item, the sixth known item, the seventh known item, and the eighth known item.

6. After completing the rehearsal sequence with the first item, that first unknown item is then treated as the first known, the previous eighth known is removed, and a new unknown item is introduced. Thus, the number of cards in this example always remains nine.

7. Continue individually rehearsing unknown items until three errors occur while rehearsing one item. Errors need not only occur on the item currently being rehearsed. Any inability to state an item correctly within 3 seconds counts as an error, even if that error occurs on a previously rehearsed item or an item that was known before the sequence began.

correct, then repeat these steps until it is spelled correctly. Erase the model and what the student wrote, and rehearse the unknown word with the sequence presented in Table 7.5.

Reading Fluency

Once a lack of consistency between instructional material and student skill is identified with CBA-ID, task difficulty can be modified to meet the needs of the individual student. For example, teachers and school psychologists can conduct a series of 1-minute CBA-ID to identify a series of reading material that can be used for instruction. Selecting material that represents an instructional level will increase comprehension, completion, and time on task during instruction (Gickling & Armstrong, 1978; Treptow et al., 2007). However, teachers should carefully monitor reading skills to be sure that the identified books/reading material still represents an instructional level after providing intervention.

Special education teachers and interventionists often have the flexibility to find or create different reading material for individual students. However, that is not often the case in general education classrooms, and CBA-ID can be used to preteach the unknown words to "elevate the passage to an instructional level" (Gravois & Gickling, 2002, p. 895). Previewing reading material before completing an assigned task has consistently led to better reading fluency and comprehension among children with and without disabilities (Burns, Dean, & Foley, 2004; Rose, 1984; Shapiro, 1992).

Word Search

Words can be pretaught by first conducting a word search to identify known and unknown words within the reading passage, teaching unknown words, and assessing progress within the reading curriculum. We suggest identifying the material that will be used for reading instruction that day (e.g., pages in a basal or an authentic text) and sitting down with the student. Say to the student, "I am going to ask you to read some words to me. When I point to a word, please read it out loud to me. Do your very best. Some words will be hard and some should be easy. Any questions? Let's begin." Next, point to words that the student likely cannot read and ask him or her to read the word. Words that are correctly read within 2 seconds are considered known and those that are incorrectly read or correctly read beyond 2 seconds are considered unknown. In addition, as recommended by Gravois and Gickling (2008), every third word pointed to should be one that the student could read easily in order to ensure that enough known words are found and to keep the activity from being too frustrating.

Record the known and unknown words in the Word Search form included in Appendix A. Keep identifying unknown and known words until there are 8–10 known words. The number of unknown words will vary based on the student's acquisition rate (AR). Use information from previous assessments to determine the number of unknown items that you will need. If the student's previous AR was 5, then identify seven unknown words to preteach. The additional two words are identified just in case they are needed. If this is the first time working with the student, then an estimate can be made based on previous research. Burns (2004a) found an average AR of 3 for first grade, 5 for third grade, and 7 for fifth grade. Again, it is probably better to identify more unknown words than what will likely be needed.

It may be beneficial to target particular words. For example, assume that the student's reading was sampled from a 200-word passage that will be used in class. If the student correctly read 90% of the words correctly, that would be 180 words or 20 unknown words. In our experience, we have never encountered a student of any age who could be taught 20 words in one session. Therefore, it is beneficial to focus on words that appear more frequently or are central to the meaning of the text. We suggest avoiding vocabulary words and so on that only appear once.

Intervention

After generating a list of unknown words and nine known words, the student is taught the unknown words with IR as described in Table 7.5. Each words is written in ink on a 3″ × 5″ index card. Present the first unknown word to the student, verbally provide the correct pronunciation, and ask the student to orally restate the word and use it in a sentence. If the student does not correctly use the word in a sentence, then he or she is provided a definition and a correct use of the word in a sentence, and then asked to verbally use the word in a different sentence. Finally, rehearse the unknown word with the sequence in Table 7.5. After completing this sequence, the first unknown word is treated as the first known, the previous final known word is removed, and a new unknown word is introduced.

Some might wonder why IR should be used for this intervention because there are other previewing methods and approaches to teaching words. However, previous research found IR to be more effective than other drill models containing 100% unknown words and 50% unknown words (MacQuarrie et al., 2002) and to be an effective preteaching strategy for children identified as having a learning disability (LD) in reading (Burns, 2007; Burns, Dean, & Foley, 2004). Moreover, IR has been consistently demonstrated to be superior to other flash-card methods (Kupzyk, Daly, & Andersen, 2011). There are less intensive approaches than IR, and we recommend that intervention efforts in Tiers 1 and 2 rely on less intense and more efficient approaches. However, if a student requires a Tier 3 intervention, then that warrants focusing on effectiveness versus efficiency, which suggests that IR is appropriate.

Research has consistently demonstrated that preteaching words in the manner described here resulted in increased student learning. In one study, we pretaught unknown words from the grade-level curriculum with students identified as having an LD in reading and found that they progressed at a rate in reading that not only outperformed the control group but also outperformed their peers without disabilities (Burns, 2007). Moreover, we correlated the growth rate for each student with the number of times that the student read the instructional material at an instructional level after preteaching, and the correlation was $r = .80$. Therefore, how well each student learned was directly related to being able to read the material and instructional level. Preteaching is a simple intervention that only takes a few minutes, but has powerful implications.

Reading Comprehension

Much of the focus of this book is on code-based aspects of reading, such as fluency and decoding, but reading comprehension skills among middle and high school students are at a critical low (RAND Reading Study Group, 2002), and reading instruction among middle and high school students is primarily focused on vocabulary and comprehension (Kamil et al., 2008). Reading interventions for struggling readers are an important aspect of effective reading comprehension, and interventions most often involve supportive instruction in vocabulary and explicit reading comprehension strategies (Torgesen, Houston, & Rissman, 2007). However, comprehension strategies have smaller effects for middle school students than high school students (Scammacca et al., 2007) and strategy instruction is only one aspect of literacy instruction among adolescent readers (Torgesen et al., 2007).

Reading comprehension is more affected by background knowledge and vocabulary than use of specific comprehension strategies (Cromley & Azevedo, 2007). Moreover, poor comprehenders often lack sufficient background knowledge to understand what they read (Gersten, Fuchs, Williams, & Baker, 2001) because comprehension involves creating mental representations of the text and using those representations to interpret the text (Pressley & Afflerbach, 1995). The two common approaches to help students better develop mental representations before reading are previewing the text (Graves, Cooke, & LaBerge, 1983) and preteaching key words (Burns, Dean, & Foley, 2004).

Previewing

Previewing is often accomplished by asking the student questions about the topic, providing a synopsis of the story, repeating the names of the characters, and defining three or four difficult words before the student reads the material. Previous research found that middle school struggling readers answered 67% of the comprehension questions correctly after previewing, but those who did not preview answered only 58% correctly (Graves et al., 1983).

Graves and colleagues (1983) outlined previewing procedures to address two major components: short questions and statements designed to engage students with the text, and a synopsis of main story elements. The short questions and statements should be related to themes or ideas presented in the text. The next aspect is to describe all of the major story elements: setting, characters, point of view (narration), and description of the plot. Next, the names and descriptions of main characters should be clearly written on white, unlined 3″ × 5″ index cards, which are presented to the students during the previewing intervention.

Key Words

Although previewing is a commonly used method to help students develop mental representations, background knowledge can also be enhanced by preteaching words that are central to the meaning of the text. There is a close relationship between vocabulary and comprehension (National Reading Panel, 2000), and preteaching can directly enhance vocabulary knowledge for the text.

Previous research found that students identified as learning disabled in reading answered 34% of comprehension questions correctly without preteaching, but answered 58% correctly after preteaching (Burns, Dean, & Foley, 2004). However, preteaching key words was less frequently studied among middle and high school students. A direct comparison of previewing and preteaching key words with middle school students found that preteaching was significantly more effective than previewing (Burns, Hodgson, et al., 2011).

Preteaching key words begins by identifying the key words. We suggest examining the text to be used for instruction. This is an important activity for reading instruction, but we frequently use this intervention for other content areas such as social studies, history, and government. Key words are defined as words that are "central to understanding the meaning of the reading passage" (Rousseau & Yung Tam, 1991, p. 201). The key words are written on a 3″ × 5″ index card and are presented to the student in much the same way described above. The student is again asked to read the word within 2 seconds, and is asked to use the word in a sentence. Correctly reading the word is only one-half of identifying it as a known item. The student must also provide a sentence in which the word is used in a manner that is semantically correct. If the student does not read the word within 2 seconds, then it is an unknown, but if he or she also does not provide a correct sentence, then it is also considered an unknown.

Many teachers and school psychologists rely on vocabulary lists provided by various curricula, but we recommend against doing so. We recently were preteaching key words from a social studies textbook to a group of high school students and simply used the bolded vocabulary words as the key words. One of the words that we pretaught was *communism* and the students learned the word with little difficulty. However, when they attempted to read the words in context, we realized that although they could read and understand the word *communism*, they could not read the word *government*, and if you cannot read the word *government*, then reading the word *communism* will not facilitate comprehension. We also noted that the bolded vocabulary words only appeared once and the text was written such that the definition of the words was included in the text. Thus, we suggest focusing on words that are central to understanding the reading, which are often not the bolded curriculum-identified vocabulary words.

Once enough known and unknown words are identified (see above), then the words are taught using IR as shown in Table 7.5. Students read and rehearse a short definition for each unknown word every time it is presented. Teachers, school psychologists, and other interventionists should lightly write a synonym or two- to three-word definition for each word on the back of the index card. Then, every time the word is presented, the student should orally state the word and its corresponding definition. Provide the student the correct definition every time that he or she does not correctly state it.

The link between reading fluency and comprehension is well established, and many fluency interventions have strong effects on comprehension as well (Therrien, 2004). However, it may be necessary to focus on vocabulary and background knowledge to increase comprehension, which can be accomplished by conducting a CBA-ID and preteaching unknown key words. It should be noted that the interventions for fluency and comprehension presented here are not instructional strategies. We have had many conversations with school district directors of curriculum and instruction about what constitutes effective reading instruction because many object to using flash cards or to teaching words. Our response to that is that (1) there is an extensive research base to support the effectiveness of flash card approaches; and (2) we are not teaching students to read, we are simply getting them ready to receive reading instruction.

Interventions and instruction are actually synergistic. Neither intervention presented here for reading connected text will provide much benefit unless the student is also participating in effective reading instruction. However, if the instructional task requires the student to read text in which he or she can only read 85% of the words, or does not understand the words that he or she reads, then the student will likely not complete the task, will not comprehend or benefit from the instruction, and will be off task during instruction. A simple 5- to 10-minute intervention before reading instruction occurs will greatly enhance the effectiveness of the instruction.

Letter Sounds

CBA-ID can also be used to assess discrete skills such as letter sounds, but it becomes less curriculum based because the universe of assessment items is no longer specific to the curriculum. In other words, there are only 26 letters in the English language and they will be taught in almost all reading curricula. Thus, if known and unknown sounds are identified with CBA-ID (see Chapter 4) and the student correctly responds to less than 90% of the letters, then they can be taught in a manner at the student's instructional level.

Letter sounds can be taught with IR using the procedures outlined above and having the student provide the letter sound every time that it is presented. However, Volpe and colleagues (Volpe et al., 2011) used a continuous string of letter sounds presented on one sheet of paper to teach letter sounds to kindergarten students who did not learn the sounds from other approaches. Begin by presenting the unknown letter to the student and saying "This is a [letter name] and it makes the [letter sound] sound. What sound does it make?" Most students correctly respond with the first try, but the steps are repeated if the student makes an error. After repeating the correct sound for the letter three times with scaffolding and feedback from the interventionists three times, they then read a page of letters and are instructed to "Say the sound for each letter." In the following example, the underlined letter is the new letter and the other letters not underlined are known. However, do not underline the target letter in practice, we did so here for a clearer demonstration.

<u>s</u>   m   <u>s</u>   m   r   <u>s</u>   m   r   t   <u>s</u>   m
r   t   n   <u>s</u>   m   r   t   n   d

There is one unknown item (*s*) and five known items. The student is rehearsing the unknown in the same way that IR is conducted, interspersing with known items and increasing the number of known items between presentation of the unknown by one time. After the student reads the lines above, a second letter is practiced by adding it before each *s* and deleting the letter *d*.

Math

There are not as many interventions for math as there are for reading, but meta-analytic research has identified important components of an effective intervention. First, intensive interventions for math should use principles of explicit instruction in teaching both math concepts and procedures (Baker et al., 2002), and computation interventions should include practice with modeling and various approaches to providing high repetition with the task (Codding, Burns, & Lukito, 2011).

CBA-ID can be used to assess procedural skill within specific objectives (see above and Chapter 5) and to assess conceptual understanding (Chapter 5). It would go beyond the scope of this book to discuss interventions for conceptual understanding because those interventions are not based on CBA-ID. Readers are referred to the work of Van De Walle (e.g., Van De Walle et al., 2010) to find interventions to enhance conceptual understanding. Here we briefly discuss IR for math and the interspersal technique.

IR for Math

Because we have already discussed IR in great detail, we will not do so again here. Previous research found that using IR significantly increased the math skills of students with math difficulties (Burns, 2005; Codding et al., 2010). The IR procedure would be the same as outlined in Table 7.5. Students would be asked to state the equation and the answer every time that the unknown item was presented, but would only say the answer for known items.

Interspersal

Interspersal is an instructional technique in which easier discrete tasks are placed within sets of target tasks, which consistently led to increased task preference for mathematics assignments (Cates & Skinner, 2002; Logan & Skinner, 1998) and higher completion rates for tasks of greater difficulty (McDonald & Ardoin, 2007). However, interspersal does little to increase the accuracy with which the target problems are completed and should be used to provide additional practice and not initial learning.

Interspersal is consistent with the concept of an instructional level because it involves including known items within a learning task to increase time on task. However, it should only be used within the context of the learning hierarchy (see Chapter 2). Students should not be allowed to practice something independently until they can complete the task with high accuracy (at least 85–90% for math tasks). Thus, it would be best to teach the student the concepts and steps in the procedures until they complete the task accurately, then provide them independent practice to build fluency with the skill so that they can generalize it and use the skill to solve problems (Haring & Eaton, 1978).

Interspersal can be a method for students to practice applying basic skills to more advanced ones. For example, if the student is being asked to complete an assignment regarding triple-digit multiplication, then interspersing easier items (e.g., single-digit multiplication) would likely increase the probability that the students would complete the task. Most approaches to interspersing involve placing the easy item every second, third, or fifth problem. Meta-analytic research found that drill approaches with less than 50% known were not effective. Thus, we suggest incorporating an easy item (e.g., single-digit multiplication) in between every other target problem (triple-digit multiplication) so that the ratio of easy to target would be 50%. If 50% does not seem to be effective enough, then try adding two (66%) or three (75%) easy problems for every target problem. It is important to note that the problems should be added and not replaced. Do not reduce the number of target items to rehearse because practice is important, just add easy items in, which will make the assignment appear longer, but if the easy problems can be completed quickly from memory, then adding them in will not take much longer to complete the assignment and will significantly increase the likelihood that it is completed.

Writing

There are even fewer Tier 3 interventions for writing than there are for reading and math, but research has begun to identify assessment approaches that complement and incorporate CBA-ID data. Once students have the skill to proficiently transcribe their ideas on paper, intervention should focus on equipping students with the self-regulatory skills to be able to plan, organize, monitor, and revise their writing (Graham & Harris, 2009). CBA-ID data can indicate if students have reached a proficient skill level, and our opinion is that most Tier 3 problems are related to students who are attempting to use transcription skills they do not have (e.g., they either have not acquired accurate spelling and handwriting skills, or they have not developed proficient levels of those skills). Therefore, CBA-ID data can be used to target interventions based on more individualized and analytic assessments.

Parker, Dickey, and colleagues (2012) used CBA-ID data to generate individualized hypotheses for why three first graders were exhibiting poor writing skills that were nonresponsive to previous intervention efforts. Based on the CBA-ID data all three students were identified as having instructional-level transcription skills, meaning they had developed the skill to accurately demonstrate handwriting and spelling skills, but those skills were not proficient. Therefore, multiple intervention approaches were tested using a more intensive, functional assessment approach called brief experimental analysis. The analysis briefly tested interventions using choice, incentives, and repeated practice to determine which approach (or combination) would be successful in improving student skills. An intervention approach involving modeling was also tested to ensure students did not need additional modeling to build accurate transcription skills. The results of the additional assessment were used to individualize interventions to each student's unique needs (all of which needed a proficiency-focused intervention), which is consistent with the need for further assessment and analysis at Tier 3 of RTI (Burns, Deno, & Jimerson, 2007).

Burns, Ganuza, and London (2009) also used additional assessment and analysis to identify an effective writing strategy for a struggling student. Although CBA-ID procedures were not directly used, the student was producing extremely short writing samples with correct letter formation as little as 50% of the time. This student was likely experiencing considerable frustration with writing, and the evidence suggested his skills were at the frustration level. Thus, not surprisingly, of the interventions that were tested, the one that included explicit modeling of letter formation produced the strongest effects, and those effects transferred to all taught letters.

CONCLUSION

Many schools are using grade-level teams to implement a multi-tiered system of support. However, many grade-level teams struggle to identify common assessments, criteria with which to judge student proficiency, and a process to collaboratively analyze data and improve student learning (DuFour, Eaker, & DuFour, 2005; Love, 2009), which is concerning because data-based decision making is at the core of effective MTSS models.

CBA-ID provides the framework for collecting, interpreting, and using data to drive instruction and intervention. Tier 1 decisions can be made by using data to group children and provide additional practice reading instructional-level material. Tier 2 decisions can be made by using CBA-ID data to target interventions to a general area such as reading decoding, comprehension, math objectives, or transcription skills such as spelling. Finally, CBA-ID data can be used to develop individualized interventions that have been shown to work well even with the most severely challenged students. Thus, CBA-ID provides a research-based approach to improve instruction and intervention within a grade-level team model.

> **CBA-ID provides the framework for collecting, interpreting, and using data to drive instruction and intervention.**

CHAPTER 8

CBA-ID in Action

We both are fortunate to have jobs that allow us to spend much of our time working in K–12 schools, interacting with special and general education teachers, school psychologists, interventionists, reading specialists, and reading teachers, and directly working with children. Below are some examples of times that we, or people with whom we have worked, have used CBA-ID in research or in intervention efforts. All of the names are pseudonyms, and the data are based on actual data, but are changed or simulated to protect the anonymity of the students on which they are based.

READING WITH A THIRD-GRADE STUDENT

Greg was a student in a third-grade classroom who attending Williams Elementary School. He had good attendance and was a hard worker, but he was beginning to demonstrate behavioral difficulties. His time on task during reading instruction ranged from 50 to 75%, and his teacher indicated that Greg's behavior was starting to interfere with his learning and that reinforcement systems were not working. Thus, Greg was referred for a special education evaluation because of reading difficulties. His IQ fell in the low average range (IQ between 80 and 90) and his achievement scores fell between the 10th and 16th percentiles for his age group. His intelligence and achievement were commensurate and he was not recommended for a special education support.

We hypothesized that Greg's behavioral difficulties were the direct result of frustration during reading instruction. Greg's reading skills were assessed with CBA-ID by taking three 1-minute assessments from his classroom reading basal. The median fluency rate and percentage of words read correctly were recorded. The percentage of words read correctly were 80%, 85%, and 72% and his fluency rates were 30 words/minute, 33 words/minute, and 24 words/minute, respectively.

Daily intervention consisted of determining the reading lessons for the week and finding the unknown words through a word search. Next, a peer tutor taught Greg the unknown words each morning using incremental rehearsal (IR) with seven known words. His acquisition rate (AR) was 4, so approximately four words were taught each day (three to five), and the peer tutoring sessions ranged from approximately 5 to 15 minutes each morning.

We monitored progress each week with CBA-ID using the classroom basal, but also monitored progress with a weekly curriculum-based measurement (CBM) using third-grade probes from Aimsweb (2006). Figure 8.1 displays Greg's data. He went from reading 72 to 85% correct before we began the intervention, but he was quickly reading more than 93% of the words correctly. His behavioral difficulties also improved dramatically. His time on task increased to consistently over 90% and we noticed that he was again raising his hand to answer questions and choosing to read during free times.

Greg completed the state test in April of this third-grade year. He was identified as a student who would likely not pass the state test when we first started working with him. The great news is that Greg did pass the state test in third grade, which we celebrated with him.

The intervention continued in fourth grade, but was reduced to twice weekly and practicing high-frequency words. His progress was monitored only once each month, and showed continued growth.

MATH WITH A FOURTH-GRADE GENERAL EDUCATION STUDENT

A second example of CBA-ID with a general education student is presented for Wayne, who attended Schafer Elementary as a fourth grader. Wayne was discussed at a building-level

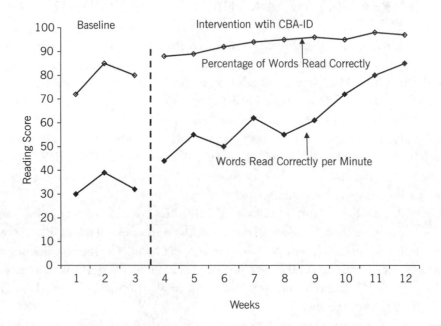

FIGURE 8.1. Oral reading fluency data for Greg while receiving an intervention based on CBA-ID.

problem-solving team meeting because of a lack of progress in learning multiplication facts. Dr. Huiskens, the school psychologist, started monitoring Wayne's progress each week with timed multiplication-fact CBM probes consisting of single-digit multiplication facts. He completed 45–75% correct, and his digits correct per minute (DCPM) ranged from 3 to 12.

Wayne's baseline scores consisted of 3, 12, and 9 DCPM. His classroom teacher had been using math manipulatives to reteach the concept of multiplication for about 2 weeks, but with little progress. Therefore, Dr. Huiskens used the Conceptual Understanding Interview (Chapter 5) to assess Wayne's understanding of the underlying concepts. Wayne received a score of 20, which suggested that he understood the underlying concepts, but struggled recalling the facts. At that point, the conceptual intervention stopped and the teacher assigned a peer tutor to teach Wayne the single-digit multiplication facts with IR. The peer tutor was taught IR and the two students were together taught the procedure for the intervention. The teacher observed the intervention the first two sessions, but they worked independently after that with only occasional monitoring from the teacher.

The intervention sessions occurred three times each week. The peer tutor used eight known facts each time and Wayne's AR was 5, but the number of unknown facts taught in a session ranged from four to six. Each session began with a review of the facts that were taught last time. Facts that were correctly answered within 2 seconds of presentation were considered known and were used as known items during the intervention session. Those that were not correctly answered within 2 seconds were retaught. The intervention sessions required approximately 10 minutes each.

Wayne's progress was monitored with weekly single-digit multiplication probes. He completed one probe each week for 2 minutes. The number of DCPM was recorded and used to monitor progress. As shown in Figure 8.2, Wayne scored within the frustration-

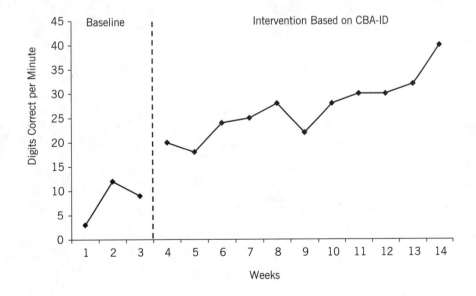

FIGURE 8.2. Wayne's digits correct per minute on single-digit multiplication CBA-ID probes during intervention.

level range during baseline, but his data quickly reached the instructional level of 24–49 DCPM and eventually fell within the independent range. At that point, the intervention was stopped.

MATH CONCEPTS WITH A SECOND-GRADE STUDENT

Tom was an 8-year-old Caucasian male attending second grade at Kreucher Elementary School. His teacher reported that Tom had substantial difficulties with math and reading. He scored at the 15th percentile on the group-administered measure of math skills and received Title 1 support for reading, but no additional assistance for math. Kreucher Elementary is an urban school with a student population that was less than 50% white and more than 50% eligible for the federal free or reduced-price lunch program.

The teacher reported that Tom struggled with double-digit addition. Mr. Fridline, the school psychologist, conducted a CBA-ID with single-digit addition that contained 40 math problems with a vertical orientation in eight rows of five each on worksheets. The assessment probes were created with *www.mathfactcafe.com*. Tom was given 2 minutes to complete as many problems as he could and the data were converted to a DCPM metric.

Tom's CBA-ID scores fell within the frustration range (i.e., less than 14 DCPM), and Mr. Fridline suggested that the teacher implement IR with the addition facts three times per week. Before beginning the intervention, Tom averaged about 8 DCPM. As can be seen in Figure 8.3, implementing IR was not effective and the average DCPM in this phase was about 7.5. Thus, we conducted a conceptual assessment to determine whether Tom under-

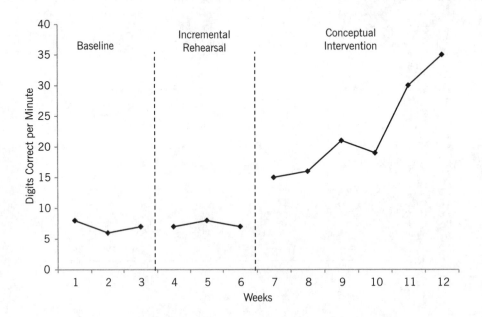

FIGURE 8.3. Tom's digits correct per minute on single-digit addition CBA-ID probes during the incremental rehearsal and conceptual interventions.

stood the concepts upon which addition are based. The conceptual assessment contained 20 single-digit addition problems that were presented with pictorial representations of the problems (e.g., $3 + 4 = 7$ was represented by two circles with three dots in one and four dots in the other; see Chapter 5 and Appendix C). A total of 20 single-digit addition picture problems were written on a sheet with two examples in each line, one that was correct and one that was incorrect. The incorrect problems had one extra or one too few objects in one of the two circles. Tom completed the worksheet by circling the problem that was correct within each pair of problems.

The conceptual understanding assessments for Thomas occurred three times on 3 different days with no time limit. He circled the correct answer 10 out of 20 times on the first sheet, 12 out of 20 on the second, and 6 out of 20 for the third, which equaled a total of 28 of 60 (47%) items correctly answered. Thus, Tom's answers closely approximated chance and it was concluded that he did not demonstrate sufficient conceptual understanding of single-digit addition on the assessments.

The conceptual intervention for Tom involved visual representation of the problem with physical manipulative objects, as recommended by the National Council of Teachers of Mathematics (2000). Thus, we modeled the addition of single-digit problems with small green plastic blocks that physically linked to one another and by following addition lessons from Learning Resources (n.d.). Each lesson involved modeling the number of blocks that matched a written single-digit addition equation, and using the blocks to solve the equation by counting. After modeling how to match the written number to a number of green blocks, Tom would be given an addition problem and would first find the number of blocks that matched the written numbers in the equation. He then counted the blocks to solve the equation. Finally, he was allowed to practice completing equations with the blocks.

We monitored progress with weekly CBA-ID with single-digit addition. Baseline data were collected for 3 weeks, and IR was implemented for 3 weeks. Finally, we implemented the conceptual intervention and monitored progress for 4 weeks. Intervention sessions were conducted four times each week. A classroom paraprofessional implemented the interventions one-on-one while sitting at a small desk outside of the classroom in an open area off of the main hallway. One intervention session occurred per day and lasted approximately 15 minutes each, but occurred at different times throughout the day depending on the day of the week. However, the intervention always occurred outside of core math instruction time.

During the conceptual intervention, Tom's scores improved from approximately 8 DCMP in baseline and 7.5 for IR to an average over 30. Baseline and IR data had 100% overlap, but all of the data in conceptual intervention exceeded the baseline and IR data.

MATH CONCEPTS WITH A MIDDLE SCHOOL STUDENT WITH A MATH LEARNING DISABILITY

Jill was an eighth-grade African American female student attending a middle school in a large urban district. She was diagnosed with a learning disability in math in fifth grade. Her most recent special education disability identification evaluation found an IQ that fell within the low end of the average range (percentile ranks of 40th to 45th), reading skills that fell within the low average range (percentile ranks of 25th to 35th), but math skills that fell at the 6th percentile. Her most recent individualized education plan (IEP) included goals that address math computation and reducing fractions.

Jill participated in a special education math course for 1 hour each day, but did not receive any other special education support. Mr. Tarzell was Jill's special education teacher who worked with her toward her IEP goals. He expressed a concern because Jill was not mastering basic concepts for fractions, but was progressing well with other computation aspects of math. Jill correctly completed about 50% of the items on most recent assessments for adding fractions with like denominators, despite Mr. Tarzell trying "everything" with her.

We began by conducting a CBA-ID for math concepts. Jill was given two assessments that each contained a sheet with 20 items. Each item had two fractions and a pie chart. She was instructed to circle the fraction that went with the picture (Chapter 5), much like the example shown below.

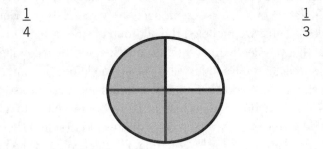

$$\frac{1}{4} \qquad\qquad\qquad\qquad \frac{1}{3}$$

Jill circled the correct fraction for the picture 45% of the time on the first assessment, and 50% of the time on the second, which approximated chance and indicated that she was probably guessing. These percentages were also below the 85–90% criterion for the instructional level and suggested that she did not understand the underlying concept. We also administered a brief assessment provided by the special education teacher that assessed reducing fractions with 10 open-answer problems. She did not correctly complete any of the problems.

The intervention began with direct instruction in the concept of fractions. We provided Jill a series of pie charts like the one shown above and modeled counting the number of wedges in which the pie chart was divided, counting the number of highlighted or open wedges, and using that to determine a fraction. We modeled the first one for her, and then asked her to restate our steps. We then gave her a second pie chart and asked her to complete the task on her own, but monitored her closely and gave feedback at every step. We then gave her a series of 5–10 pie charts that she completed independently. After she demonstrated success on three straight independent practices, all on 3 different days, then we moved to more complex fractions such as 3/4, 5/8, 4/7, and 9/10. We monitored her progress by giving her a sheet like the one demonstrated above, but with randomly selected fractions from 1/2 to 9/10. As can be seen in Figure 8.4, she started out at approximately 50%, but reached 100% after just three sessions.

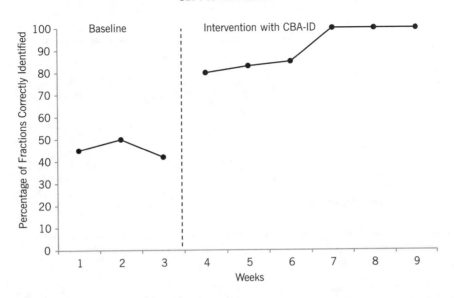

FIGURE 8.4. Percentage of correct answers on the CBA-ID fraction assessment for Jill.

After Jill had learned the concept of fractions, we taught her the concept of reducing fractions. We did so with a factor tree like the one shown below.

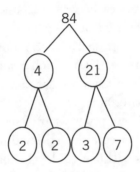

She met one-on-one with an interventionist three times each week and during the session a number with a blank factor tree was completed by the interventionist to model the process. The exact same blank factor tree was given to Jill with the same number at the top and the same number of empty circles, and she completed it on her own with feedback from the interventionist. Finally, she was given 5–10 blank factor trees to complete while the interventionist gave feedback.

Jill was taught factor trees for three sessions, and then we taught her how to reduce fractions with the factors by again modeling it, having her redo what we completed, completing one on her own with immediate feedback, and then giving her problems for independent practice. We also ended each session with a 2-minute assessment in which she was given a series of 20 fractions and asked to reduce each to the lowest common denominator. The data from those assessments are included in Figure 8.5. She correctly answered 100% and scored within the instructional-level range for DCPM by the third session.

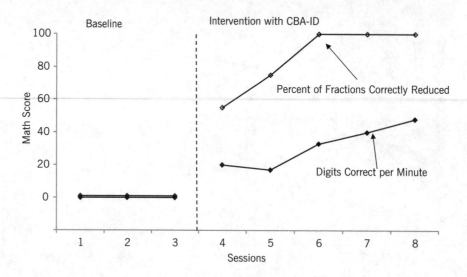

FIGURE 8.5. Jill's digits correct per minute on the CBA-ID probes that addressed reducing fractions.

DECODING WITH A SECOND-GRADE STUDENT

Michael was a Hispanic second grader who was diagnosed with a reading disability in first grade. His special education teacher used daily repeated reading sessions with instructional-level books and self-monitoring of progress. His instructional level was assessed with a commonly used informal reading inventory (IRI), which resulted in a reading level of F, which translates to a primer level. Reading fluency assessments fell well below the 10th percentile for his age group on grade-level material.

Michael was not making sufficient progress after several weeks. The teacher was concerned about his reading level. Therefore, we assessed his reading skills with books produced by the same publisher as the IRI using F-level books. We conducted a CBA-ID with three F-level books and the percentage of words read correctly ranged from 75 to 85%. Therefore, the F-level books did not appear to represent an instructional level for Michael.

We followed up the CBA-ID with the F-level books with an assessment of Michael's phonetic skills with a list of low-frequency highly decodable words (Chapter 4) using CBA-ID procedures. He correctly identified less than 90% of the sounds, which suggested that he required additional support with learning his letter sounds and other decoding skills. Therefore, the teacher reduced emphasis on repeated reading and increased focus on teaching letter sounds and other decoding skills. Michael received direct instruction in decoding each day that ended with contextual reading of the sounds that were taught that day.

Michael's phonetic skills were monitored with weekly letter–sound assessments. As shown in Figure 8.6, he quickly obtained the 90% known criterion on three consecutive assessments, after which the focus switched to practicing the use of letter sounds to make words with various blending activities and connected text. Also as shown in Figure 8.6,

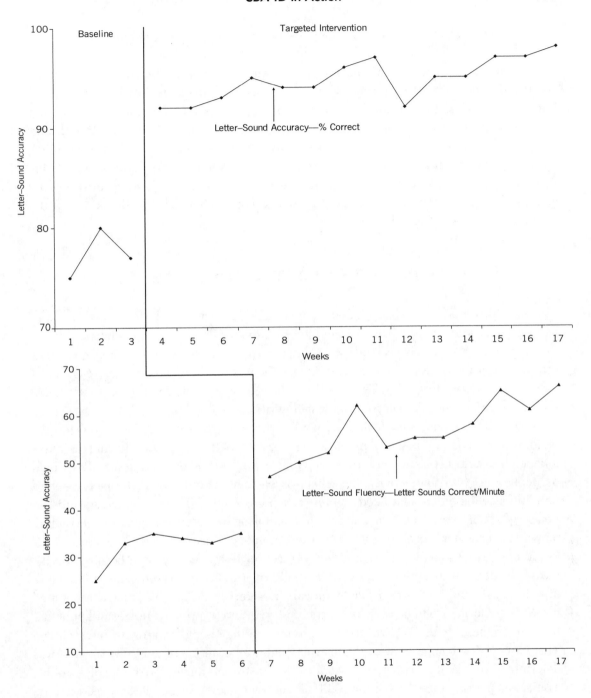

FIGURE 8.6. Percentage of letters read correctly and letter–sound fluency for Michael.

Michael's letter–sound fluency scores increased substantially after switching the intervention.

We worked closely with Michael for some time, but our involvement reduced as he continued to progress. We returned the fall of Michael's third-grade year and again asked him to read to us so that we could conduct a CBA-ID. We asked if he remembered us, and he unconvincingly claimed that he did. We then reminded him that we worked with him on reading and would like to do so again right now, to which he responded "Yeah, reading!" He then excitedly gathered his stuff and sought out a book to read. We told this story to his first- and second-grade teachers who recalled with us how much he used to resist reading and how he seemed to dread even opening a book. His teachers were so thankful that the world of reading was opened to him.

WRITING WITH A FIRST-GRADE STUDENT

Will was a first-grade boy who attended Dennison Elementary School. He worked hard and had a great attitude, but he demonstrated poor writing skills relative to his peers. Even at the beginning of the school year, he wasn't able to write as much, or with as much quality, as the other students in his classroom. After 4 weeks he was referred to the school psychologist for help with his writing skills. The first thing the school psychologist did was to use CBA-ID data to determine Will's current skills with writing.

The CBA-ID data were collected with picture–word prompts. To administer the picture–word prompt, the school psychologist met with Will for 5 minutes during his class's independent writing time. After introducing himself to Will and explaining that they would be doing a brief writing activity, the school psychologist administered the picture–word prompt following the standardized administration procedures. These included administration scripts, a brief practice item, and careful monitoring so that no more than 10 seconds of nonwriting behavior was observed during the 3 minutes of writing.

Will's writing sample was scored for correct word sequences (CWS) because, unlike measures such as words written or correctly spelled words, CWS is a more nuanced measure of writing skill and it has defensible technical characteristics. The CWS metric accounted for Will's performance in capitalization, spelling, verb usage, pronoun usage, and punctuation. He produced four CWS within the 3-minute writing sample prior to any intervention. That number was compared with the instructional-level criterion of 8–14 CWS, and it was determined that Will's writing skills were in the frustration range. Further analysis of his assessment performance showed that Will did not write many words, but those he did write were spelled accurately. His performance showed that he struggled to produce accurately formed letters and words within a sentence.

Based on the CBA-ID data, Will was provided an intervention focused on handwriting transcription skills that included a high degree of modeling, explicit instruction, and immediate feedback. It was based on the principles of cover–copy–compare (CCC), an intervention with strong research support for modeling academic skills to struggling students (Skinner, McLaughlin, & Logan, 1997). CCC was conducted during a 15-minute session one to two times a week for a total of 20 weeks.

In each CCC session, the school psychologist asked Will to select a word from his class's weekly spelling list. Then the school psychologist and Will jointly came up with a child-appropriate sentence that included the word. Next, the school psychologist wrote the sentence on lined paper and pointed out the features of a correct sentence while writing (e.g., pointing to the capital letter to start the sentence, pointing to spaces between words, pointing to action word for verbs). Next, Will used the school psychologist's version to copy the sentence while the school psychologist immediately corrected errors using standard error correction procedures. The error correction procedures consisted of the experimenter correctly modeling the sentence feature and having the student rewrite the feature. After writing the sentence with the school psychologist's model, Will wrote the sentence a second time from memory. Once Will finished copying the sentence from memory, the school psychologist uncovered the model sentence, and the student and experimenter compared the model and the student's copied sentence for similarities and differences. Again, feedback was given using the standard error correction process described above.

Figure 8.7 shows the ongoing progress data collected before and after Will began working with the school psychologist. The baseline phase lasted 4 weeks, and clearly shows that Will was not successfully acquiring writing skills in the context of the classroom instruction. After week 4, the school psychologist conducted CBA-ID and then implemented the CCC intervention with explicit instruction and modeling that the CBA-ID results indicated would best address Will's frustration-level skills. The CCC intervention was then implemented for 15 weeks, by which time Will's writing skills had reached the instructional level. Although data were not collected after that point, another CBA-ID would have been conducted to determine the best intervention approach for Will because of the success he had experienced with the CCC intervention.

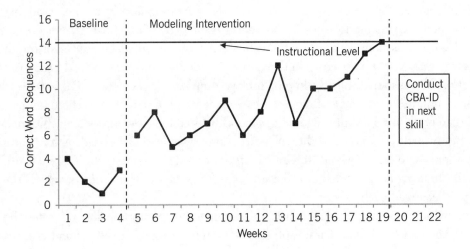

FIGURE 8.7. Correct word sequences for weekly writing assessments to monitor Will's progress.

READING CLASSWIDE

The previous examples were for individual students, but we frequently apply CBA-ID data to groups within an assessment-to-intervention framework. Lincoln Elementary is an urban K–5 elementary school that served 325 students, and it is an example of a setting where we used group data to make decisions. A total of 90% of the students who attended Lincoln Elementary were African American, 8% were white, and 2% were Asian. A total of 85% of the students were eligible for the federal free or reduced-price lunch program. The example that we will share is from the third grade. There were two third-grade classrooms with 55 students, and classwide intervention occurred in Ms. Smith's room. Ms. Smith was a third-year teacher with 24 students, 13 (54%) of whom were male and 22 (92%) were African American.

The school used CBM to conduct benchmark assessments three times per year. All students were individually assessed with three oral reading fluency passages, with the median of the three being the seasonal benchmark score for each student. The class median for the January assessment was 85 words read correctly per minute (WRCM), which was below the seasonal benchmark criterion of 91 WCM. Thus, the grade-level team determined that there was a classwide need. They decided to follow up with CBA-ID to determine an intervention plan.

Each student was assessed with a low-frequency but highly decodable word list created from the local curriculum. Each student was individually assessed for 1 minute and the number of sounds that were correctly read within each word was recorded (Chapter 4). The percentage of sounds read correctly in that minute was divided by the total number of sounds and multiplied by 100 to equal a percentage. The median percentage correct was 95.5%, which was above the instructional-level criterion of 90%. There were eight students who read less than 90% of the sounds correctly, and they were targeted for additional support in the classroom on decoding skills.

Next, the percentage of words read correctly was computed from each student's oral reading fluency assessment. Those who scored below 93% or above 97% were further assessed with classroom reading material to determine an instructional level for the set of passages that would be used for intervention. Students were then paired based on their instructional level so that they could read intervention passages together. The reading dyads met for 15 minutes each day for 2 weeks. Students worked in pairs to read text. One student would read orally for 5 minutes while the second student followed along. The students were trained to provide a standardized error correction procedure as needed. After 5 minutes, the partners switched roles and the second student read the same text aloud for 5 minutes while the first reader provided appropriate error correction. The order in which the students read changed each time.

Following the partner read, each student engaged in paragraph shrinking for the section that he or she had read. Paragraph shrinking involves having the students summarize the main idea of what they had read in 10 words or fewer. The students were taught to state the "who," "what," and "why" of the passage; they were told to put a finger down for each word of their summary, and they were to stop after placing down 10 fingers. Paragraph shrinking procedures were modeled each day at the beginning of the lesson.

The first 2 days were dedicated to training the students on the partner reading procedures. The teacher modeled the procedures for finding their materials and transitioning to the activity, partner reading, error correction, and paragraph shrinking. Setup procedures involved having each dyad gather their materials out of a bin of folders and moving to a specific spot in the classroom. Days 3 through 10 involved having the students engage in the partner reading and paragraph shrinking. Although other procedures were not modeled every day, paragraph shrinking was still modeled by the teacher each day. The intervention procedures were twice observed by the school psychologist to assess integrity and provide feedback.

Each student was again assessed with oral reading fluency following the 2-week classwide intervention. A class median was obtained from the student posttest data, which was then compared with the class pretest median to assess the effects of the intervention. The class median score increased from 85 to 109 WRCM, which was a 24 WRCM increase over 2 weeks. Moreover, the second assessment fell above the seasonal benchmark criterion of 91. The number of students who required intervention fell from 13 out of 24 (54%) to 5 of 24 (8%), which is a much more reasonable number to engage in small-group interventions.

After the classwide intervention ended, Ms. Smith decided to continue to include a daily partner reading activity for her classroom. The five students who still fell below the benchmark standard received a small-group intervention that addressed reading decoding.

MATH SCHOOLWIDE

Porter Elementary is a K–5 building located in the southeast portion of the country and had a high percentage of English language learners, 70% of the students were Caucasian, 25% were Hispanic or Latino, 4% were African American, and less than 1% were Native American. A total of 11% of the students in the building received special education services, and 13% were eligible for Title I services. There were four classrooms per grade level with approximately 25 students per class. The teachers ranged in experience from 1 to 25 years.

All students in the school were assessed in the fall, winter, and spring with two math probes, one that addressed specific skills (CBA-ID) and one to track math growth (CBM). Mathematics probes were administered to the entire class simultaneously and required about 5 minutes to complete each time.

Screening data were used to determine whether or not a classwide problem existed. If a classwide problem did exist, then classwide interventions were implemented before beginning interventions for individual students. A classwide problem was identified when the median CBM score for the class fell below the instructional level of 14 DCPM for second and third grade, and 24 DCPM for older students. In this particular school, a classwide problem was identified in every single classroom!

After the fall screening in which classwide problems were identified in all classrooms, we engaged in a series of single-skill CBA-ID to determine where to begin the intervention efforts. We started at the first objective in that grade's curriculum, which was Harcourt Math (Harcourt, 2003), and conducted a single-skill CBA-ID for that skill with a 40-problem probe that was administered as a group for 2 minutes. The median DCPM for the first objective scored in the instructional-level range for all classrooms, and additional assessments were conducted for the second, third, fourth objectives, and so on, until the median score for the classroom fell within the frustration range (i.e., below the instructional-level range). The intervention began with the highest objective that scored within the instructional-level range. For example, the students from one third-grade classroom scored within the instructional-level range for mixed addition and subtraction problems with answers 0–18 (Objective 2), but scored within the frustration-level range for three-digit addition (Objective 3). Therefore, the intervention focused on the former.

The intervention occurred within the general education classroom, and was based on work by VanDerHeyden and colleagues (VanDerHeyden & Burns, 2005b) in which concentrated practice opportunities in basic computational skills were used to build skill. The students in each classroom were divided into tutoring pairs for 15 minutes each day. Each dyad was given a set of flash cards with the target problems on the cards. The dyads rehearsed practicing the cards with a brisk pace, how to provide immediate corrective feedback, and how to look up the correct answer. After completing the flash cards, each student returned to his or her own desk and completed independent timed practice in the skill. The timed independent practice sheets were collected and scored, and when the median score exceeded the highest end of the instructional level range for three consecutive sessions, the class then moved to the next skill level.

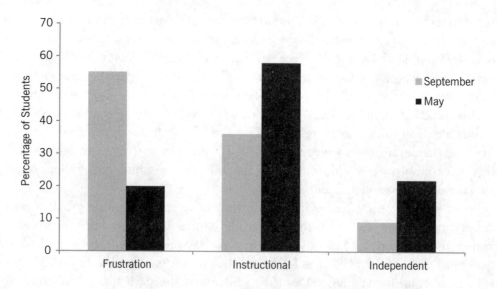

FIGURE 8.8. Digits correct per minute on CBMs for Ms. Smith's classroom at two seasonal benchmark assessments.

An intervention protocol was developed and provided to teachers that specified each step of the intervention in observable terms. The teacher's primary role was to monitor the intervention to ensure that the students were engaged and following the intervention steps. The school psychologist supported the intervention effort by giving the written procedures to the teachers, modeling them for each individual teacher, and being on hand during the first day for each classroom to assist in training the students. The intervention began in October and was implemented 4 days per week, and assessments occurred each Friday.

The school psychologist randomly selected one class each week to visit and observe for implementation integrity. The intervention was observed with an intervention protocol and the teacher was given feedback regarding implementation immediately following the intervention session. The number of steps observed being correctly implemented was recorded and the data were provided to the principal on a weekly basis.

The CBM data for the year are presented in Figure 8.8. The students made substantial progress over the course of the year and eventually scored above the benchmark criterion. Individual student data were also interpreted by using the CBA-ID data. In September, there were 55% of children who scored within the frustration range across all grades. An additional 9% fell within the independent range and 36% were in the instructional-level range. In May, the numbers changed substantially with only 20% scoring within the frustration range, 58% in the instructional range, and 22% in the independent category. It is also worth noting that the number of students who passed the state accountability test for math increased from 52% the previous year to 70% the year in which the classwide interventions were implemented.

Glossary of Abbreviations

AR: acquisition rate

CBA: curriculum-based assessment

CBA-ID: curriculum-based assessment for instructional design

CBM: curriculum-based measurement

CBM-M: curriculum-based measurement for math

CBM-R: curriculum-based measurement for reading

CBM-W: curriculum-based measurement for writing

CCC: cover–copy–compare

CCSS: Common Core State Standards

CWS: correct word sequences

DCPM: digits correct per minute

EPM: errors per minute

GOM: general outcome measure

IA: instructional assessment

IEP: individualized education plan

IH: instructional hierarchy

IR: incremental rehearsal

IRA: International Reading Association

IRI: informal reading inventory

LD: learning disability

MAP: measures of academic progress

MTSS: multi-tiered system of support

NCTE: National Council of Teachers of English

NCTM: National Council of Teachers of Mathematics

NMAP: National Math Advisory Panel

NRP: National Reading Panel

NWF: nonsense word fluency

ORF: oral reading fluency

PLC: professional learning community

PSF: phoneme segmentation fluency

RTI: response to intervention

SMM: subskill master measure

SRSD: self-regulated strategy development

WCPM: words read correctly per minute

WSC: words spelled correctly

WW: words written

Appendices

APPENDIX A. CBA-ID FOR READING

APPENDIX B. CBA-ID FOR MATH PROCEDURES

APPENDIX C. CBA-ID FOR MATH CONCEPTS

APPENDIX D. CBA-ID FOR WRITING

Assessment of Contextual Reading
PROCEDURES

1. Select a reading sample that represents the instructional material.

2. Photocopy the sample to serve as a protocol.

3. Provide the student with the reading material and say:

   "Start right here and please read this out loud so that I can hear you. Do your very best reading. If you come to a word that you don't know, I'll tell it to you. Keep reading until I tell you to stop. Ready? Begin."

4. Have the student read for 1 minute and record errors on your protocol.

5. At the end of the minute, tell the student to stop reading.

6. Words are counted as correct if they are correctly pronounced within 2 seconds, and incorrect if they are omitted, pronounced incorrectly, or pronounced correctly but after 2 seconds.

7. Count the number of words read correctly and record that above. Count the number of errors and record that number above.

8. Compute the percentage of words read correctly by dividing the number of words read correctly by the total number of words (words read correctly plus errors), and multiplying by 100.

9. Select two different samples of the same reading material (e.g., different pages from the section of the book that will be read or used for instruction that day) and repeated Steps 1–8 until you have three samples of the behavior.

10. Circle the median percentage of words read correctly. Is it within 93–97%? If so, then this material represents an instructional level. If the percentage is more than 97%, then this material represents an independent level for reading. If the percentage is less than 93%, then easier material should be selected or enough words should be pretaught so that the student can read 93% of the words correctly.

From Matthew K. Burns and David C. Parker (2014). Copyright by The Guilford Press. Permission to photocopy this material is granted to purchasers of this book for personal use only (see copyright page for details). Purchasers can download and print additional copies of this material from *www.guilford.com/burns2-forms*.

Contextual Reading Data Recording Sheet

Student Name _____

Grade _____

Date	Reading material (e.g., book and page #)	Sample 1			Sample 2			Sample 3		
		Words correct	Errors	%	Words correct	Errors	%	Words correct	Errors	%

Comments:

_____

_____

From Matthew K. Burns and David C. Parker (2014). Copyright by The Guilford Press. Permission to photocopy this material is granted to purchasers of this book for personal use only (see copyright page for details). Purchasers can download and print additional copies of this material from *www.guilford.com/burns2-forms*.

Sample Contextual Reading Data Recording Sheet

Student Name _Jimmy_   Grade _2_

Date	Reading material (e.g., book and page #)	Sample 1			Sample 2			Sample 3		
		Words correct	Errors	%	Words correct	Errors	%	Words correct	Errors	%
1–18	Holt People Need People, Pages 32, 46, 38	60	5	92	68	8	90	58	8	88
1–22	Holt People Need People, Pages 48, 55, 40	70	7	91	74	8	87	65	5	93
1–25	Holt People Need People, Pages 51, 44, 39	66	5	93	70	9	88	67	6	92
1–26	Holt People Need People, Pages 54, 41, 49	78	7	92	80	5	94	86	4	96

Comments:

119

From Matthew K. Burns and David C. Parker (2014). Copyright by The Guilford Press. Permission to photocopy this material is granted to purchasers of this book for personal use only (see copyright page for details). Purchasers can download and print additional copies of this material from *www.guilford.com/burns2-forms*.

Word Search

PROCEDURES

1. Identify known and unknown words by pointing to words in the text and asking the student to read the word.

2. Start by saying:

   "We are going to read some words. Please read the words that I point to. Some will be harder and some will be easier. Do your very best to read each word. Any questions? Let's start."

3. Point to the word and say: "What is this word?"

4. Words that are read within 2 seconds of presentation are counted as correct. Words are considered incorrect if they are pronounced incorrectly, or pronounced correctly but after 2 seconds.

5. Be sure to point to a word that is likely easy for the student at least every third word so that the task is not too frustrating.

6. Keep repeating Steps 3–5 until you identify five to eight known words and enough unknown words to reach the student's acquisition rate.

7. Record the words read correctly and incorrectly and record them below.

Based on Gravois and Gickling (2008).

From Matthew K. Burns and David C. Parker (2014). Copyright by The Guilford Press. Permission to photocopy this material is granted to purchasers of this book for personal use only (see copyright page for details). Purchasers can download and print additional copies of this material from *www.guilford.com/burns2-forms*.

Word Search Data Recording Sheet

Student Name _____ Grade _____

Date	Reading sample	Known words	Unknown words
	Sample 1:		
	Sample 2:		
	Sample 3:		
	Sample 4:		
	Sample 5:		

Comments: _____

_____

From Matthew K. Burns and David C. Parker (2014). Copyright by The Guilford Press. Permission to photocopy this material is granted to purchasers of this book for personal use only (see copyright page for details). Purchasers can download and print additional copies of this material from *www.guilford.com/burns2-forms*.

Sample Word Search Data Recording Sheet

Student Name _Jimmy_ _____ Grade _2_ _____

Date	Reading sample	Known words	Unknown words
1–18	**Sample 1:** _Holt, People Need People, Little Wolf—Pages 32 to 36_	sun sky little plants you boy fox he	wolf wise animal grandfather hunter brave morning tribe
1–25	**Sample 2:** _Holt, People Need People, The Drought—Pages 48 to 52_	town river boat dry cloud wet happy rain	summer drought farmers helicopter harvest grow
	Sample 3:		
	Sample 4:		
	Sample 5:		

Comments: _____

_____

From Matthew K. Burns and David C. Parker (2014). Copyright by The Guilford Press. Permission to photocopy this material is granted to purchasers of this book for personal use only (see copyright page for details). Purchasers can download and print additional copies of this material from _www.guilford.com/burns2-forms_.

Assessment of the Acquisition Rate

PROCEDURES

1. Find unknown and known words either through a word search or from oral reading and write them on index cards.

2. Teach the words with incremental rehearsal.

3. Count any error made by the student. Errors include incorrect pronunciation, not responding when presented with the word, or correct response after 2 seconds of presentation.

4. Keep adding in unknown words until the student makes three errors while rehearsing any one word. The errors may occur for a target word, a previously taught word, or a known word.

5. After the student makes three errors while rehearsing any one word, stop the assessment.

6. Shuffle the words that were taught and show each one final time. Ask the student to read the word when you show the card. Words that are read correctly within 2 seconds of presentation are considered known. Words not correctly read or read correctly after 2 seconds of presentation are considered unknown.

7. Count the number of known words, which equals the acquisition rate.

8. Test for retention at least 1 day later by repeating Step 6.

From Matthew K. Burns and David C. Parker (2014). Copyright by The Guilford Press. Permission to photocopy this material is granted to purchasers of this book for personal use only (see copyright page for details). Purchasers can download and print additional copies of this material from *www.guilford.com/burns2-forms*.

APPENDIX A8

Acquisition Rate Data Recording Sheet

Student Name _____ Grade _____

Date	Words taught	Date	Words retained
	1. 2. 3. 4. 5. 6. 7. 8. 9. 10. AR =		1. 2. 3. 4. 5. 6. 7. 8. 9. 10.
	1. 2. 3. 4. 5. 6. 7. 8. 9. 10. AR =		1. 2. 3. 4. 5. 6. 7. 8. 9. 10.
	1. 2. 3. 4. 5. 6. 7. 8. 9. 10. AR =		1. 2. 3. 4. 5. 6. 7. 8. 9. 10.

Notes: _____

_____

From Matthew K. Burns and David C. Parker (2014). Copyright by The Guilford Press. Permission to photocopy this material is granted to purchasers of this book for personal use only (see copyright page for details). Purchasers can download and print additional copies of this material from *www.guilford.com/burns2-forms*.

Sample Acquisition Rate Data Recording Sheet

Student Name _Jimmy_   Grade _2_

Date	Words taught	Date	Words retained
1–18	1. animal 2. hunter 3. wolf 4. grandfather 5. 6. 7. 8. 9. 10. **AR = 4**	1–19	1. animal 2. hunter 3. wolf 4. grandfather 5. 6. 7. 8. 9. 10.
1–25	1. drought 2. summer 3. farmers 4. harvest 5. 6. 7. 8. 9. 10. **AR = 4**	1–26	1. drought 2. summer 3. farmers 4. harvest 5. 6. 7. 8. 9. 10.
	1. 2. 3. 4. 5. 6. 7. 8. 9. 10. **AR =**		1. 2. 3. 4. 5. 6. 7. 8. 9. 10.

Notes: _____

_____

From Matthew K. Burns and David C. Parker (2014). Copyright by The Guilford Press. Permission to photocopy this material is granted to purchasers of this book for personal use only (see copyright page for details). Purchasers can download and print additional copies of this material from _www.guilford.com/burns2-forms_.

Assessment of Low-Frequency Decodable Words

PROCEDURES

1. Select a list of words. See the next page and also *www.cehd.umn.edu/reading/PRESS/docs/ assessments/06.Kindergarten-Word-Identification-Fluency-General-Outcome-Measure.pdf* for potential lists to use.

2. Say to the student:

   "Here is a list of words. Start at the top [point to first word], and read them out loud going this way [point left to right]. Do your very best reading and try all of the words. Keep reading until I tell you to stop. Any questions? Begin."

3. Start the timer.

4. Record any sounds that the student does not read correctly by placing a slash through them.

5. After 1 minute, say "Stop."

6. Count the number of sounds read correctly and errors for each line.

7. Count the total number of sounds read correctly and errors.

8. Divide the total number of sounds read correctly by the total number of sounds attempted (Read Correctly/[Read Correctly + Errors]) and multiply by 100 to get a percentage.

9. At least 85–90% correct is an instructional level.

From Matthew K. Burns and David C. Parker (2014). Copyright by The Guilford Press. Permission to photocopy this material is granted to purchasers of this book for personal use only (see copyright page for details). Purchasers can download and print additional copies of this material from *www.guilford.com/burns2-forms*.

Low-Frequency Decodable Word List—Student Version

wig	jam	yep
gap	sup	gad
bop	yup	bud
cop	sap	hog
pun	yap	tab
din	vet	cog
bob	hip	pox
nip	fax	ram
mod	dab	rag
fib	sop	jot
con	fad	cub
tug	bet	den
lit	fix	fog
rig	cod	jig
sod	lab	mot

From Matthew K. Burns and David C. Parker (2014). Copyright by The Guilford Press. Permission to photocopy this material is granted to purchasers of this book for personal use only (see copyright page for details). Purchasers can download and print additional copies of this material from *www.guilford.com/burns2-forms*.

Low-Frequency Decodable Words Recording Sheet

Student Name _____   Grade _____

			Correct	Total
wig	jam	yep	_____	9
gap	sup	gad	_____	9
bop	yup	bud	_____	9
cop	sap	hog	_____	9
pun	yap	tab	_____	9
din	vet	cog	_____	9
bob	hip	pox	_____	9
nip	fax	ram	_____	9
mod	dab	rag	_____	9
fib	sop	jot	_____	9
con	fad	cub	_____	9
tug	bet	den	_____	9
lit	fix	fog	_____	9
rig	cod	jig	_____	9
sod	lab	mot	_____	9

Totals: _____

Total Correct _____   **Total Correct + Errors** _____   **Percentage** _____

Notes: _____

_____

From Matthew K. Burns and David C. Parker (2014). Copyright by The Guilford Press. Permission to photocopy this material is granted to purchasers of this book for personal use only (see copyright page for details). Purchasers can download and print additional copies of this material from *www.guilford.com/burns2-forms*.

Sample Low-Frequency Decodable Words Recording Sheet

Student Name _Greg_ _____ Grade _____

			Correct	Total
wig	j̸am	y̸ep	7	9
gap̸	sup̸	gad	7	9
bop	y̸up	bud	8	9
cop	sap	ho̸g̸	7	9
pu̸n	y̸ap	tab	7	9
dj̸n	vet	cog̸	7	9
bob	hip	pox	9	9
nj̸p	fax	ram	8	9
mod	dab	ra̸g	8	9
fib	sop	jot	9	9
con	fad	cub	9	9
tug	bet	den		9
lit	fix	fog		9
rig	cod	jig		9
sod	lab	mot		9
	Totals:		86	99

Total Correct _86_ _____ **Total Correct + Errors** _99_ _____ **Percentage** _87%_ _____

Notes: _Vowel errors were all reading them with long sounds. Said /j/ sound for y._
_____

From Matthew K. Burns and David C. Parker (2014). Copyright by The Guilford Press. Permission to photocopy this material is granted to purchasers of this book for personal use only (see copyright page for details). Purchasers can download and print additional copies of this material from *www.guilford.com/burns2-forms*.

Assessment of Math Procedures

PROCEDURES

1. Select the math objective to begin the assessment. If the student scores in the instructional-level range, then stop. If the student scores in the frustration-level range, then assess the next lower math objective. If the student scores in the independent range, then assess the next more difficult objective.

2. Select or create a probe that assesses the objective.

3. Place the math probe in front of the student and say:

   "Please complete these problems. Look at each problem carefully before answering. Start with the first problem and work across the page. Try all of the problems, but place an X over problems that you do not know how to do. Keep working until you finish or until I tell you to stop. Any questions? Please begin." (based on Shinn & Shinn, 2004)

4. Give the students 2 minutes (first through third grade) or 4 minutes (fourth grade and older) to complete the probe. Have the student read for 1 minute and record errors on your protocol.

5. When the time expires, tell the student: "Stop and put your pencil down."

6. Collect the probe and score it by counting all of the digits correct.

7. Divide the number of digits correct by the total number of minutes (2 or 4) to compute a digits correct per minute (DCPM) score.

8. Compare the DCPM score to the following criteria:

Grade	Frustration	Instructional	Independent
1–3	0–13	14–31	32 or higher
4th and above	0–23	24–49	50 or higher

From Matthew K. Burns and David C. Parker (2014). Copyright by The Guilford Press. Permission to photocopy this material is granted to purchasers of this book for personal use only (see copyright page for details). Purchasers can download and print additional copies of this material from *www.guilford.com/burns2-forms*.

APPENDIX B2

Math Procedures Data Recording Sheet

Student Name _____   Grade _____

Date	Objective	Sample 1			Sample 2			Sample 3		
		DCPM	Errors	%	DCPM	Errors	%	DCPM	Errors	%

Comments: _____

From Matthew K. Burns and David C. Parker (2014). Copyright by The Guilford Press. Permission to photocopy this material is granted to purchasers of this book for personal use only (see copyright page for details). Purchasers can download and print additional copies of this material from *www.guilford.com/burns2-forms*.

Conceptual Assessment for Single-Digit Computation

Student Name _____ Grade _____ Date _____

Look at the picture of dots below the two problems and circle the problem that best goes with the picture.

1. 2 + 4 = 6   3 + 4 = 7

2. 4 + 2 = 6   4 + 1 = 5

3. 6 + 5 = 11   6 + 3 = 9

4. 5 + 2 = 7   5 + 3 = 8

5. 4 + 5 = 9   4 + 6 = 10

6. 3 + 2 = 5   3 + 4 = 7

7. 4 + 4 = 8   6 + 4 = 10

8. 2 + 1 = 3   4 + 1 = 5

9. 2 + 5 = 7   3 + 5 = 8

(continued)

From Matthew K. Burns and David C. Parker (2014). Copyright by The Guilford Press. Permission to photocopy this material is granted to purchasers of this book for personal use only (see copyright page for details). Purchasers can download and print additional copies of this material from *www.guilford.com/burns2-forms*.

10. 6 + 6 = 12 6 + 2 = 8

11. 3 + 6 = 9 4 + 6 = 10

12. 3 + 2 = 5 4 + 2 = 6

13. 4 + 2 = 6 1 + 6 = 7

14. 6 + 5 = 11 4 + 5 = 9

15. 3 + 2 = 5 5 + 3 = 8

16. 2 + 1 = 3 4 + 1 = 5

17. 4 + 5 = 9 5 + 5 = 10

18. 4 + 3 = 7 4 + 4 = 8

19. 6 + 6 = 12 5 + 6 = 11

20. 3 + 2 = 5 2 + 2 = 4

Total correct: _____ of 20 (Instructional level = 16–18)

Conceptual Understanding Interview

Problem 1

Please draw a picture that goes with the problem below, and use the picture to solve the problem.

$$2 \times 4 = \underline{\hspace{2cm}}$$

Problem 2

Please draw a picture that goes with the problem below, and use the picture to solve the problem.

$$3 \times 6 = \underline{\hspace{2cm}}$$

From Matthew K. Burns and David C. Parker (2014). Copyright by The Guilford Press. Permission to photocopy this material is granted to purchasers of this book for personal use only (see copyright page for details). Purchasers can download and print additional copies of this material from *www.guilford.com/burns2-forms*.

Sample Conceptual Understanding Interview

Problem 1

Please draw a picture that goes with the problem below, and use the picture to solve the problem.

$$2 \times 4 = \underline{\qquad}$$

○ ○ × ○ ○ ○ ○ = 8

Problem 2

Please draw a picture that goes with the problem below, and use the picture to solve the problem.

$$3 \times 5 = \underline{\qquad}$$

☺ ☺ ☺ × ○ ○ ○ ○ ○ = 15

From Matthew K. Burns and David C. Parker (2014). Copyright by The Guilford Press. Permission to photocopy this material is granted to purchasers of this book for personal use only (see copyright page for details). Purchasers can download and print additional copies of this material from *www.guilford.com/burns2-forms*.

Interview Questions

Student Name _____ Grade _____ Date _____

Ask the students the following questions and write down their answer as close to verbatim as you can. If needed, answers can be further probed with the following two follow-up questions:

"Please tell me more about what you did so I can understand you better."

"I never thought about it that way. Can you tell me more?"

1. How did you figure out this problem?

2. How did you find the answer?

Please tell me more.

3. What do [point to pictures/objects] you mean and how did they help you solve the problem?

4. Tell me what you were thinking in your head when you were doing this.

5. How did you check your answer to see if it was correct?

From Matthew K. Burns and David C. Parker (2014). Copyright by The Guilford Press. Permission to photocopy this material is granted to purchasers of this book for personal use only (see copyright page for details). Purchasers can download and print additional copies of this material from *www.guilford.com/burns2-forms*.

Sample Interview Questions

Student Name <u>Rich</u>　　　　　　　Grade <u>Third</u>　　　Date <u>March 12</u>

Ask the students the following questions and write down their answer as close to verbatim as you can. If needed, answers can be further probed with the following two follow-up questions:

"Please tell me more about what you did so I can understand you better."

"I never thought about it that way. Can you tell me more?"

1. How did you figure out this problem?

    Counted the threes and the fives.

2. How did you find the answer?

    Added them up.

    Please tell me more.

    Used the pictures to solve it.

3. What do [point to pictures/objects] you mean and how did they help you solve the problem?

    They are pictures. They are happy like are me.

4. Tell me what you were thinking in your head when you were doing this.

    Multiplication

5. How did you check your answer to see if it was correct?

    Go back and do it again.

From Matthew K. Burns and David C. Parker (2014). Copyright by The Guilford Press. Permission to photocopy this material is granted to purchasers of this book for personal use only (see copyright page for details). Purchasers can download and print additional copies of this material from *www.guilford.com/burns2-forms*.

Student Response Scoring Sheet

Student Name _____ Grade _____ Date _____

Criterion	Unsatisfactory Task is attempted, but little or no success	Partial Part of the items is demonstrated, but no evidence of understanding	Proficient Only minor errors and adequate understanding of the item to complete the task	Excellent Complete understanding to accomplish item
1. Counts with understanding	1	2	3	4
2. Understands the number sign	1	2	3	4
3. Understands the facts of adding/ subtracting or multiplication/ division of whole numbers	1	2	3	4
4. Correctly uses the visual model (i.e., there was a correct relationship between the diagram that the student created and the problem)	1	2	3	4
5. Uses an identifiable strategy	1	2	3	4
6. Answers the problem correctly	1	2	3	4

Comments: _____

_____

_____

_____

Total score: _____ of 24 (Instructional level = 20–22)

From Matthew K. Burns and David C. Parker (2014). Copyright by The Guilford Press. Permission to photocopy this material is granted to purchasers of this book for personal use only (see copyright page for details). Purchasers can download and print additional copies of this material from www.guilford.com/burns2-forms.

Sample Student Response Scoring Sheet

Student Name *Rich*   Grade *Third*   Date *March 12*

Criterion	Unsatisfactory Task is attempted, but little or no success	Partial Part of the items is demonstrated, but no evidence of understanding	Proficient Only minor errors and adequate understanding of the item to complete the task	Excellent Complete understanding to accomplish item
1. Counts with understanding	1	2	3	(4)
2. Understands the number sign	1	(2)	3	4
3. Understands the facts of adding/ subtracting or multiplication/ division of whole numbers	1	(2)	3	4
4. Correctly uses the visual model (i.e., there was a correct relationship between the diagram that the student created and the problem)	1	(2)	3	4
5. Uses an identifiable strategy	(1)	2	3	4
6. Answers the problem correctly	1	2	3	(4)

Comments: *Seemed to count correctly and answered the problem correctly. Also seemed to understand that multiplication meant combining groups to get a bigger number, but did not use any identifiable strategy. Is likely guessing or has memorized the answers.*

Total score: *15*   of 24 (Instructional level = 20–22)

From Matthew K. Burns and David C. Parker (2014). Copyright by The Guilford Press. Permission to photocopy this material is granted to purchasers of this book for personal use only (see copyright page for details). Purchasers can download and print additional copies of this material from *www.guilford.com/burns2-forms*.

Assessment Writing

PROCEDURES

1. Select a writing task that represents the curricular objectives. See *www.progressmonitoring.org/probes/earlywriting.html* for examples.

2. Photocopy the task to serve as a protocol.

3. Provide an explanation of task expectations, and any necessary directions for the specific task being completed.

4. Provide the student with the writing task and say:

   "Put your pencil on the first line. When I say 'begin,' start writing at top left [point to where] of the first line. If you don't know how to spell a word, just try your best. Do your best work and keep writing until I say 'Stop.'"

   Make sure students are ready to start and say: "Please begin writing."

5. Have the student write for 3 minutes. If the student stops writing for more than 10 seconds, say, "Keep writing until I say 'Stop.'"

6. At the end of the 3 minutes, tell the student to stop writing.

7. Score the writing task for correct word sequences, words spelled correctly, or words written. See *www.progressmonitoring.org/probes/earlywriting.html* or access additional scoring procedures from commercial products (e.g., *www.aimsweb.com*).

8. Count the number of word sequences, words spelled correctly, or words written and record below.

9. Compare the scores to the following criteria (correct word sequences shown below; see Parker, McMaster, & Burns, 2011, for other scoring metrics):

Task	Frustration	Instructional	Independent
Sentence copying	0–9	10–16	17 or higher
Picture–Word	0–7	8–14	15 or higher

From Matthew K. Burns and David C. Parker (2014). Copyright by The Guilford Press. Permission to photocopy this material is granted to purchasers of this book for personal use only (see copyright page for details). Purchasers can download and print additional copies of this material from *www.guilford.com/burns2-forms*.

Writing Data Recording Sheet

Student Name _____   Grade _____

Date	Task (e.g., probe #)	Sample 1			Sample 2			Sample 3		
		CWS	Errors	%	WSC	Errors	%	WW	Errors	%

Comments:

_____

From Matthew K. Burns and David C. Parker (2014). Copyright by The Guilford Press. Permission to photocopy this material is granted to purchasers of this book for personal use only (see copyright page for details). Purchasers can download and print additional copies of this material from *www.guilford.com/burns2-forms*.

References

Adams, M. J. (1990). *Beginning to read: Thinking and learning about print.* Cambridge, MA: Harvard University Press.

Aimsweb. (2006). *Measures/norms.* Eden Prairie, MN: Edformation.

Aimsweb. (2010). *Measures/norms.* Bloomington, MN: Pearson.

Alber-Morgan, S. R., Ramp, E. M., Anderson, L. L., & Martin, C. M. (2007). Effects of repeated readings, error correction, and performance feedback on the fluency and comprehension of middle school students with problem behavior. *Journal of Special Education, 41,* 17–30.

Algozzine, R., Ysseldyke, J., & Elliott, J. (1997). *Strategies and tactics for effective instruction* (2nd ed.). Longmont, CO: Sopris West.

Allington, R. L. (2009). If they don't read much . . . 30 years later. In E. H. Hiebert (Ed.), *Reading more, reading better* (pp. 30–54). New York: Guilford Press.

American Educational Research Association, American Psychological Association, & National Council on Measurement in Education. (1999). *Standards for educational and psychological assessment.* Washington, DC: American Psychological Association.

Appleton, J. J., Christenson, S. L., Kim, D., & Reschly, A. L. (2006). Measuring cognitive and psychological engagement: Validation of the student engagement instrument. *Journal of School Psychology, 44,* 427–445.

Archer, A., Flood, J., Lapp, D., & Lungren, L. (2011). *Phonics for reading.* North Billerica, MA: Curriculum Associates.

Archer, A., Gleason, M., & Vachon, V. (2006) *REWARDS reading excellence: Word attack and rate development strategies.* Longmont, CO: Sopris West.

Ardoin, S. P., & Daly, E. J. III. (2007). Close encounters of the instructional kind: How the instructional hierarchy is shaping instructional research 30 years later. *Journal of Behavioral Education, 16,* 1–6.

Baker, S., Gersten, R., & Lee, D. S. (2002). A synthesis of empirical research on teaching mathematics to low-achieving students. *Elementary School Journal, 103,* 51–73.

Baker, S. K., Chard, D. J., Ketterlin-Geller, L. R., Apichatabutra, C., & Doabler, C. (2009). Teaching writing to at-risk students: The quality of evidence for self-regulated strategy development. *Exceptional Children, 75,* 303–318.

Bangert-Drowns, R. L., Hurley, M. M., & Wilkinson, B. (2004). The effects of school-based writing-to-learn interventions on academic achievement: A meta-analysis. *Review of Educational Research, 74,* 29–58.

Batsche, G., Elliott, J., Graden, J., Grimes, J., Kovaleski, J., Prasse, D., et al. (2005). *Response to intervention: Policy considerations and implementation.* Alexandria, VA: National Association of State Directors of Special Education.

Beavers, J. M. (2006). *Developmental reading assessment* (3rd ed.). Parsippany, NJ: Pearson.

Beck, M., Burns, M. K., & Lau, M. (2009). Preteaching unknown items as a behavioral intervention for children with behavioral disorders. *Behavior Disorders, 34,* 91–99.

Berninger, V., & Amtmann, D. (2003). Preventing written expression disabilities through early and continuing assessment and intervention for handwriting and/or spelling problems: Research into practice. In H. L. Swanson, K. R. Harris, & S. Graham (Eds.), *Handbook of learning disabilities* (pp. 345–363). New York: Guilford Press.

Berninger, V., Yates, C., Cartwright, A., Rutberg, J., Remy, E., & Abbott, R. (1992). Lower-level developmental skills in beginning writing. *Reading and Writing, 4,* 257–280.

Berninger, V. W., Abbott, R. D., Vermeulen, K., & Fulton, C. M. (2006). Paths to reading comprehension in at-risk second-grade readers. *Journal of Learning Disabilities, 39,* 334–351.

Berninger, V. W., Abbott, R. D., Vermeulen, K., Ogier, S., Brooksher, R., Zook, D., et al. (2002). Comparison of faster and slower responders to early intervention in reading: Differentiating features of their language profiles. *Learning Disability Quarterly, 25,* 59–76.

Berninger, V. W., Vaughan, K. B., Abbott, R. D., Abbott, S. P., Rogan, L. W., Brooks, A., et al. (1997). Treatment of handwriting problems in beginning writers: Transfer from handwriting to composition. *Journal of Educational Psychology, 89,* 652–666.

Berninger, V. W., Vaughn, K. B., Abbott, R. D., Brooks, A., Abbott, S., Reed, E., et al. (1998). Early intervention for spelling problems: Teaching functional spelling units of varying size with a multiple-connections framework. *Journal of Educational Psychology, 90,* 587–605.

Blachman, B. A., Ball, E. W., Black, R., & Tangel, D. M. (2000). *Road to the code: A phonological awareness program for young children.* Baltimore: Brookes.

Bloom, B. S., Hastings, J. T., & Madaus, G. F. (1971). *Handbook on formative and summative evaluation of student learning.* New York: McGraw-Hill.

Brainerd, C. J., & Reyna, V. F. (1995). Learning rate, learning opportunities, and the development of forgetting. *Developmental Psychology, 31,* 251–262.

Bramlett, R. K., Murphy, J. J., Johnson, J., Wallingsford, L., & Hall, J. D. (2002). Contemporary practices in school psychology: A national survey of roles and referral problems. *Psychology in the Schools, 39,* 327–335.

Bray, G. B., & Barron, S. (2003–2004). Assessing reading comprehension: The effects of text-based interest, gender, and ability. *Educational Assessment, 9,* 107–128.

Bunn, R., Burns, M. K., Hoffman, H. H., & Newman, C. L. (2005). Using incremental rehearsal to teach letter identification with a preschool-aged child. *Journal of Evidence-Based Practice for Schools, 6,* 124–134.

Burns, M. K. (2001). Measuring acquisition and retention rates with curriculum-based assessment. *Journal of Psychoeducational Assessment, 19,* 148–157.

Burns, M. K. (2002). Utilizing a comprehensive system of assessment to intervention using curriculum-based assessments. *Intervention in School and Clinic, 38,* 8–13.

Burns, M. K. (2004a). Age as a predictor of acquisition rates as measured by curriculum-based assessment: Evidence of consistency with cognitive research. *Assessment for Effective Intervention, 29*(2), 31–38.

Burns, M. K. (2004b). Empirical analysis of drill ratio research: Refining the instructional level for drill tasks. *Remedial and Special Education, 25,* 167–175.

Burns, M. K. (2004c). Using curriculum-based assessment in the consultative process: A review of three levels of research. *Journal of Educational and Psychological Consultation, 15,* 63–78.

Burns, M. K. (2005). Using incremental rehearsal to increase fluency of single-digit multiplication facts with children identified as learning disabled in mathematics computation. *Education and Treatment of Children, 28,* 237–249.

Burns, M. K. (2007). Reading at the instructional level with children identified as learning disabled: Potential implications for response-to-intervention. *School Psychology Quarterly, 22,* 297–313.

Burns, M. K. (2011). Matching math interventions to students' skill deficits. *Assessment for Effective Intervention, 36,* 210–218.

Burns, M. K., Christ, T. J., Boice, C. H., & Szadokierski, I. (2010). Special education in an RTI model: Addressing unique learning needs. In T. A. Glover & S. Vaughn (Eds.), *The promise of response to intervention: Evaluating current science and practice* (pp. 267–285). New York: Guilford Press.

Burns, M. K., Codding, R. S., Boice, C. H., & Lukito, G. (2010). Meta-analysis of acquisition and fluency math interventions with instructional and frustration level skills: Evidence for a skill-by-treatment interaction. *School Psychology Review, 39,* 69–83.

Burns, M. K., & Dean, V. J. (2005a). Effect of acquisition rates on off-task behavior with children identified as learning disabled. *Learning Disability Quarterly, 28,* 273–281.

Burns, M. K., & Dean, V. J. (2005b). Effect of drill ratios on recall and on-task behavior for children with learning and attention difficulties. *Journal of Instructional Psychology, 32,* 118–126.

Burns, M. K., Dean, V. J., & Foley, S. (2004). Preteaching unknown key words with incremental rehearsal to improve reading fluency and comprehension with children identified as reading disabled. *Journal of School Psychology, 42,* 303–314.

Burns, M. K., Dean, V. J., & Klar, S. (2004). Using curriculum-based assessment in the responsiveness to intervention diagnostic model for learning disabilities. *Assessment for Effective Intervention,* 29(3), 47–56.

Burns, M. K., Deno, S. L., & Jimerson, S. R. (2007). Toward a unified response-to-intervention model. In S. R. Jimerson, M. K. Burns, & A. VanDerHeyden (Eds.), *Handbook of response to intervention* (pp. 428–440). New York: Springer.

Burns, M. K., Ganuza, Z., & London, R. (2009). Brief experimental analysis of written letter formation: Single-case demonstration. *Journal of Behavioral Education, 18,* 20–34.

Burns, M. K., & Helman, L. (2009). Relationship between language skills and acquisition rate of sight-words among English language learners. *Literacy Research and Instruction, 48,* 221–232.

Burns, M. K., Hodgson, J., Parker, D. C., & Fremont, K. (2011). Comparison of the effectiveness and efficiency of text previewing and preteaching keywords as small-group reading comprehension strategies with middle school students. *Literacy Research and Instruction, 50,* 241–252.

Burns, M. K., Kanive, R., & DeGrande, M. (2012). Effect of a computer-delivered math fact intervention as a supplemental intervention for math in third and fourth grades. *Remedial and Special Education, 33,* 184–191.

Burns, M. K., & Kimosh, A. (2005). Using incremental rehearsal to teach sight-words to adult students with moderate mental retardation. *Journal of Evidence-Based Practices for Schools, 6,* 135–148.

Burns, M. K., Kwoka, H., Lim, B., Crone, M., Haegele, K., Parker, D. C., et al. (2011). Minimum reading fluency necessary for comprehension among second-grade students. *Psychology in the Schools, 48,* 124–132.

Burns, M. K., MacQuarrie, L. L., & Campbell, D. T. (1999). The difference between curriculum-based assessment and curriculum-based measurement: A focus on purpose and result. *Communiqué,* 27(6), 18–19.

Burns, M. K., & Mosack, J. (2005). Criterion-referenced validity of measuring acquisition rates with curriculum-based assessment. *Journal of Psychoeducational Assessment, 25,* 216–224.

Burns, M. K., Riley-Tillman, T. C., & VanDerHeyden, A. M. (2012). *RTI applications: Vol. 1. Academic and behavioral interventions.* New York: Guilford Press.

Burns, M. K., Tucker, J. A., Frame, J., Foley, S., & Hauser, A. (2000). Interscorer, alternateform, internal consistency, and test–retest reliability of Gickling's model of curriculum-based assessment for reading. *Journal of Psychoeducational Assessment, 18,* 353–360.

Burns, M. K., Tucker, J. A., Hauser, A., Thelen, R., Holmes, K., & White, K. (2002). Minimum reading fluency rate necessary for comprehension: A potential criterion for curriculum-based assessments. *Assessment for Effective Intervention, 28,* 1–7.

Burns, M. K., VanDerHeyden, A. M., & Jiban, C. (2006). Assessing the instructional level for mathematics: A comparison of methods. *School Psychology Review, 35,* 401–418.

Burns, M. K., Zaslofsky, A. F., Kanive, R., & Parker, D. C. (2012). Meta-analysis of incremental rehearsal: Using phi coefficients to compare single-case and group designs. *Journal of Behavioral Education, 21,* 185–202.

Burns, P. C., & Roe, B. D. (2007). *Informal reading inventory* (7th ed.). Boston: Houghton Mifflin.

Canobi, K., Reeve, R., & Pattison, P. E. (2003). Patterns of knowledge in children's addition. *Developmental Psychology, 39,* 521–534.

Canobi, K. C., Reeve, R. A., & Pattison, P. E. (2002). Young children's understanding of addition concepts. *Educational Psychology, 22,* 513–532.

Carnine, D. W., Silbert, J., Kame'enui, E. J., & Tarver, S. G. (2004). *Direct instruction reading* (4th ed.). Upper Saddle River, NJ: Merrill Prentice-Hall.

Cates, G. L., & Skinner, C. H. (2002). Getting remedial mathematics students to prefer homework with 20% and 40% more problems: An investigation of the strengths of the interspersing procedure. *Psychology in the Schools, 37,* 339–347.

Catts, H. W., Adlof, S. M., & Weismer, S. E. (2006). Language deficits in poor comprehenders: A case for the simple view of reading. *Journal of Speech, Language, and Hearing Research, 49,* 278–293.

Cepeda, N. J., Pashler, H., Vul, E., Wixted, J. T., & Rohrer, D. (2006). Distributed practice in verbal recall tasks: A review and quantitative synthesis. *Psychological Bulletin, 132,* 354–380.

Ceraso, J. (1967). The interference theory of forgetting. *Scientific American, 217,* 117–124.

Chall, J. S. (1983). *Stages of reading development.* New York: McGraw-Hill.

Christ, T. J. (2008). Best practices in problem analysis. In A. Thomas & J. Grimes (Eds.), *Best practices in school psychology V* (pp. 159–176). Bethesda, MD: National Association of School Psychologists.

Christ, T. J., Johnson-Gros, K. N., & Hintze, J. M. (2005). An examination of alternate assessment durations when assessing multiple-skill computational fluency: The generalizability and dependability of curriculum-based outcomes within the context of educational decisions. *Psychology in the Schools, 42,* 615–622.

Codding, R. S., Archer, J., & Connell, J. (2010). A systematic replication and extension of using incremental rehearsal to improve multiplication skills: An investigation of generalization. *Journal of Behavioral Education, 19,* 93–105.

Codding, R. S., Burns, M. K., & Lukito, G. (2011). Meta-analysis of mathematic computation fluency interventions: A component analysis. *Learning Disability Research and Practice, 26,* 36–47.

Codding, R. S., Chan-Iannetta, L., Palmer, M., & Lukito, G. (2009). Examining a classwide application of cover–copy–compare with and without goal setting to enhance mathematics fluency. *School Psychology Quarterly, 24,* 173–185.

Coker, D. L., & Ritchey, K. D. (2010). Curriculum-based measurement of writing in kindergarten and first grade: An investigation of production and qualitative scores. *Exceptional Children, 76,* 175–193.

Connor, C. M., Morrison, F. J., Fishman, B. J., Schatschneider, C., & Underwood, P. (2007). Algorithm-guided individualized reading instruction. *Science, 315,* 464–465.

Coulter, W. A., & Coulter, E. M. (1990). *Curriculum-based assessment for instructional design: Trainer's manual.* Unpublished training manual. Available from Directions and Resources, PO Box 57113, New Orleans, LA 70157.

Council for Exceptional Children Board of Directors. (2004). *The Council for Exceptional Children definition of a well-prepared special education teacher.* Reston, VA: Council for Exceptional Children.

Cowan, R., Dowker, A., Christakis, A., & Bailey, S. (1996). Even more precisely assessing children's understanding of the order-irrelevance principle. *Journal of Experimental Child Psychology, 62,* 84–101.

Cromley, J. G., & Azevedo, R. (2007). Testing and refining the direct and inferential mediation model of reading comprehension. *Journal of Educational Psychology, 99,* 311–325.

Cutler, L., & Graham, S. (2008). Primary grade writing instruction: A national survey. *Journal of Educational Psychology, 100,* 907–919.

Daly, E. J., III, Witt, J. C., Martens, B. K., & Dool, E. J. (1997). A model for conducting a functional analysis of academic performance problems. *School Psychology Review, 26,* 554–574.

Day, R., & Park, J. (2005). Developing reading comprehension questions. *Reading in a Foreign Language, 17*(1), 60–73.

Deno, S. L. (1985). Curriculum-based measurement: The emerging alternative. *Exceptional Children, 52,* 219–232.

Deno, S. L. (2003). Curriculum-based measures: Development and perspectives. *Assessment for Effective Intervention, 28*(3–4), 3–12.

Deno, S. L., & Mirkin, P. K. (1977). *Data-based program modification: A manual.* Reston, VA: Council for Exceptional Children.

Dickinson, D. J., & Butt, J. A. (1989). The effects of success and failure on the on-task behavior of high-achieving students. *Education and Treatment of Children, 12,* 243–253.

Donovan, J. J., & Radosevich, D. J. (1999). A metaanalytic review of the distribution of practice effect: Now you see it, now you don't. *Journal of Applied Psychology, 84,* 795–805.

DuFour, R. (2005). What is a professional learning community? In R. DuFour, R. Eaker, & R. DuFour (Eds.), *On common ground: The power of professional learning communities* (pp. 31–44). Bloomington, IN: Solution Tree.

DuFour, R., Eaker, R., & DuFour, R. (2005). Recurring themes of professional learning communities and the assumptions they challenge. In R. DuFour, R. Eaker, & R. DuFour (Eds.), *On common ground: The power of professional learning communities* (pp. 7–30). Bloomington, IN: Solution Tree.

Eccles, J., Adler, T. F., Futterman, R., Goff, S. B., Kaczala, C. M., Meece, J., et al. (1983). Expectancies, values and academic behaviors. In J. T. Spence (Ed.), *Achievement and achievement motives* (pp. 75–146). San Francisco: Freeman.

Ehri, L. (1998). Grapheme-phoneme knowledge is essential for learning to read words in English. In J. Metsala & L. Ehri (Eds.), *Word recognition in beginning literacy* (pp. 3–40). Mahwah, NJ: Erlbaum.

Ellis, A. K. (2005). *Research on educational innovations* (4th ed.). Larchmont, NY: Eye on Education.

Enggren, P., & Kovaleski, J. F. (1996). *Instructional*

assessment. Harrisburg: Instructional Support System of Pennsylvania.

Fein, H., Baker, S. F., Smolkowski, K., Smith, J. L. M., Kame'enui, E. J., & Beck, C. T. (2008). Using nonsense word fluency to predict reading proficiency in kindergarten through second grade for English learners and native English speakers. *School Psychology Review, 37*, 391–408.

Fountas, I. C., & Pinnell, G. S. (1996). *Guided reading: Good first teaching for all children.* Portsmouth, NH: Heinemann.

Fountas, I. C., & Pinnell, G. S. (2007). *Fountas and Pinnell benchmark assessment system 2.* Portsmouth, NH: Heinemann.

Freeland, J. T., Skinner, C. H., Jackson, B., McDaniel, C. E., & Smith, S. (2000). Measuring and increasing silent reading comprehension rates via repeated readings. *Psychology in the Schools, 37,* 415–429.

Fry, A., & Hale, S. (1996). Relationships among processing speed, working memory and fluid intelligence in children. *Biological Psychology, 54,* 1–34.

Fuchs, D., Fuchs, L. S., Mathes, P. G., & Simmons, D. C. (1997). Peer-assisted learning strategies: Making classrooms more responsive to academic diversity. *American Educational Research Journal, 34,* 174–206.

Fuchs, L., & Deno, S. (1991). Paradigmatic distinctions between instructionally relevant measurement models. *Exceptional Children, 57,* 488–500.

Fuchs, L. S., Fuchs, D., Hosp, M. K., & Hamlett, C. L. (2003). The potential for diagnostic analysis within curriculum-based measurement. *Assessment for Effective Intervention, 28*(3–4), 13–22.

Fuchs, L. S., Fuchs, D., Hosp, M. K., & Jenkins, J. R. (2001). Oral reading fluency as an indicator of reading competence: A theoretical, empirical, and historical analysis. *Scientific Studies of Reading, 5*, 239–256.

Fuchs, L. S., Fuchs, D., & Karns, K. (2001). Enhancing kindergarteners' mathematical development: Effects of peer-assisted learning strategies. *Elementary School Journal, 101,* 495–510.

Gathercole, S. E., & Baddeley, A. D. (1993). Phonological working memory: A critical building block for reading development and vocabulary acquisition? *European Journal of Psychology of Education, 8,* 259–272.

Geary, D. C., Hoard, M. K., Byrd-Craven, J., Nugent, L., & Numtee, C. (2007). Cognitive mechanisms underlying achievement deficits in children with mathematical learning disability. *Child Development, 78,* 1343–1359.

Gersten, R., Fuchs, L. S., Williams, J. P., & Baker, S. (2001). Teaching reading comprehension strategies to students with learning disabilities: A review of research. *Review of Educational Research, 71,* 279–320.

Gettinger, M., & Seibert, J. K. (2002). Best practices in increasing academic learning time. In A. Thomas & J. Grimes (Eds.), *Best practices in school psychology* (4th ed., pp. 773–788). Bethesda, MD: National Association of School Psychologists.

Gickling, E., & Rosenfield, S. (1995). Best practices in curriculum-based assessment. In A. Thomas & J. Grimes (Eds.), *Best practices in school psychology III* (pp. 587–595). Bethesda, MD: National Association of School Psychologists.

Gickling, E., & Thompson, V. (1985). A personal view of curriculum-based assessment. *Exceptional Children, 52,* 205–218.

Gickling, E. E. (1984, October). *Operationalizing academic learning time for low achieving and handicapped mainstreamed students.* Paper presented at the annual meeting of the Northern Rocky Mountain Educational Research Association, Jackson Hole, WY. (ERIC Document Reproduction Service No. ED256115)

Gickling, E. E., & Armstrong, D. L. (1978). Levels of instructional difficulty as related to on-task behavior, task completion, and comprehension. *Journal of Learning Disabilities, 11,* 559–566.

Gickling, E. E., & Havertape, S. (1981). *Curriculum-based assessment (CBA).* Minneapolis, MN: School Psychology Inservice Training Network.

Gickling, E. E., Shane, R. L., & Croskery, K. M. (1989). Developing math skills in low-achieving high school students through curriculum-based assessment. *School Psychology Review, 18,* 344–356.

Glover T. A., & Albers, C. A. (2007). Considerations for evaluating universal screening assessments. *Journal of School Psychology, 45,* 117–135.

Gough, P. B., & Tunmer, W. E. (1986). Decoding, reading, and reading disability. *Remedial and Special Education, 7,* 6–10.

Graham, S. (2013). Writing standards. In L. M. Morrow, K. K. Wixson, & T. Shanahan (Eds.), *Teaching with the Common Core Standards for English language arts, grades 3–5* (pp. 88–106). New York: Guilford Press.

Graham, S., Berninger, V. W., Abbott, R. D., Abbott, S. P., & Whitaker, D. (1997). Role of mechanics in composing of elementary school students: A new methodological approach. *Journal of Educational Psychology, 89*, 170–182.

Graham, S., & Harris, K. (2009). Almost 30 years of writing research: Making sense of it all with *The Wrath of Khan. Learning Disabilities Research, 24*, 58–68.

Graham, S., & Harris, K. R. (1994). Implications of constructivism for teaching writing to students with special needs. *Journal of Special Education, 28*, 275–289.

Graham, S., Harris, K. R., & Larsen, L. (2001). Prevention and intervention of writing difficulties for students with learning disabilities. *Learning Disabilities Research and Practice, 16*, 74–84.

Graham, S., & Perin, D. (2007). A meta-analysis of writing instruction for adolescent students. *Journal of Educational Psychology, 99*, 445–476.

Graves, M. F., Cooke, C. L., & LaBerge, M. J. (1983). Effects of previewing difficult short stories on low ability junior high school students' comprehension, recall, and attitudes. *Reading Research Quarterly, 18*, 262–276.

Gravois, T. A., & Gickling, E. (2008). Best practices in instructional assessment. In A. Thomas & J. Grimes (Eds.), *Best practices in school psychology* (Vol. IV, pp. 503–518). Bethesda, MD: National Association of School Psychologists.

Gravois, T. A., & Gickling, E. E. (2002). Best practices in curriculum-based assessment. In A. Thomas & J. Grimes (Eds.), *Best practices in school psychology* (4th ed., pp. 885–898). Bethesda, MD: National Association of School Psychologists.

Gregory, R. J. (2000). *Psychological testing: History, principles, and applications* (3rd ed.). Boston: Allyn & Bacon.

Gresham, F. M. (2002). Responsiveness to intervention: An alternative approach to the identification of learning disabilities. In R. Bradley & L. Danielson (Eds.), *Identification of learning disabilities: Research to practice* (pp. 467–519). Mahwah, NJ: Erlbaum.

Hamilton, C., & Shinn, M. R. (2003). Characteristics of word callers: An investigation of the accuracy of teachers' judgments of reading comprehension and oral reading skills. *School Psychology Review, 32*, 228–240.

Hanich, L. B., Jordan, N. C., Kaplan, D., & Dick, J. (2001). Performance across different areas of mathematical cognition in children with learning difficulties. *Journal of Educational Psychology, 93*, 615–626.

Harcourt. (2003). *Harcourt math.* Orlando, FL: Author.

Hargis, C. (2005). *Curriculum-based assessment: A primer* (3rd ed.). Springfield, IL: Thomas.

Haring, N. G., & Eaton, M. D. (1978). Systematic instructional technology: An instructional hierarchy. In N. G. Haring, T. C. Lovitt, M. D. Eaton, & C. L. Hansen (Eds.), *The fourth R: Research in the classroom* (pp. 23–40). Columbus, OH: Merrill.

Harris, K., & Graham, S. (1996). *Making the writing process work: Strategies for composition and self-regulation* (2nd ed.). Cambridge, MA: Brookline Books.

Hayes, J. (1996). A new framework for understanding cognition and affect in writing. In M. Levy & S. Ransdell (Eds.), *The science of writing: Theories, methods, individual differences, and applications* (pp. 1–27). Mahwah, NJ: Erlbaum.

Hiebert, J., & Lefevre, P. (1986). Conceptual and procedural knowledge in mathematics: An introductory analysis. In J. Hiebert (Ed.), *Conceptual and procedural knowledge: The case of mathematics* (pp. 1–27). Hillsdale, NJ: Erlbaum.

Hosp, M. K., Hosp, J. L., & Howell, K. W. (2006). *The ABCs of CBM: A practical guide to curriculum-based measurement.* New York: Guilford Press.

Houchins, D. E., Shippen, M. E., & Flores, M. M. (2004). Math assessment and instruction for students at-risk. In R. Colarusso & C. O'Rourke (Eds.), *Special education for all teachers* (3rd ed., pp. 319–357). Dubuque, IA: Kendall/Hunt.

Iaqunita, A. (2006). Guided reading: A research-based response to the challenges of early reading instruction. *Early Childhood Education Journal, 33*, 413–418.

International Reading Association & the National Council of Teachers of English. (1996). *Standards for the English language arts.* Newark, DE, & Urbana, IL: Authors.

Jenkins, J. R., & O'Connor, R. E. (2002). Early identification and intervention for young children with reading/learning disabilities. In R. Bradley, L. Danielson, & D. P. Hallahan (Eds.), *Identification of learning disabilities: Research to practice* (pp. 99–149). Mahwah, NJ: Erlbaum.

Johns, J. L. (2005). *Basic Reading Inventory: Pre-primer through grade twelve and early literacy assessments* (10th ed.). Dubuque, IA: Kendall-Hunt.

Jones, C. J. (2008). *Curriculum-based assessment: The easy way to determine response-to-intervention.* Springfield, IL: Thomas.

Juel, C. (1988). Learning to read and write: A longitudinal study of 54 children from first through fourth grades. *Journal of Educational Psychology, 80*, 437–447.

Kame'enui, E. J., & Simmons, D. C. (1990). *Designing instructional strategies: The prevention of academic learning problems.* Englewood Cliffs, NJ: Macmillan.

Kamil, M. L., Borman, G. D., Dole, J., Kral, C. C., Salinger, T., & Torgesen, J. (2008). *Improving adolescent literacy: Effective classroom and intervention practices: A practice guide* (NCEE No. 2008-4027). Washington, DC: National Center for Education Evaluation and Regional Assistance, Institute of Education Sciences, U.S. Department of Education.

Kane, M. T. (2001). Concerns in validity theory. *Journal of Educational Measurement, 38,* 319–342.

Kaplan, R. M., & Saccuzzo, D. P. (2001). *Psychological testing: Principles, applications, and issues* (5th ed.). Belmont, CA: Wadsworth/Thomson Learning.

Kilpatrick, J., Swafford, J., & Finell, B. (Eds.). (2001). *Adding it up: Helping children learn mathematics.* Washington, DC: National Academy Press.

Kupzyk, S., Daly, E. J., III., & Andersen, M. N. (2011). A comparison of two flash-card methods for improving sight-word reading. *Journal of Applied Behavior Analysis, 44,* 781–792.

LaBerge, D., & Samuels, S. J. (1974). Toward a theory of automatic information processing in reading. *Cognitive Psychology, 6,* 293–323.

Lagrou, R. J., Burns, M. K., Mizerek, E. A., & Mosack, J. (2006). Effects of text presentation on reading fluency and comprehension. *Journal of Instructional Psychology, 33,* 100–109.

Lane, K. L., Harris, K. R., Graham, S., Weisenbach, J. L., Brindle, M., & Morphy, P. (2008). The effects of self-regulated strategy development on the writing performance of second-grade students with behavioral and writing difficulties. *Journal of Special Education, 41,* 234–253.

Learning Resources. (n.d.). *Hands-on standards photo-illustrated lessons for teaching with math manipulatives grades 1–2.* Vernon Hills, IL: Author.

LeFevre, J. A., Smith-Chant, B. L., Fast, L., Skwarchuk, S. L., Sargla, E., Arnup, J. S., et al. (2006). What counts as knowing?: The development of conceptual and procedural knowledge of counting from kindergarten through grade 2. *Journal of Experimental Child Psychology, 93,* 285–303.

Leslie, L., & Caldwell, J. (2006). *Qualitative reading inventory–4.* Boston: Pearson.

Linn, R. L., & Gronlund, N. E. (2000). *Measurement and assessment in teaching* (8th ed.). Upper Saddle River, NJ: Merrill/Prentice Hall.

Linn. R. L., & Miller, M. D. (2005). *Measurement and assessment in teaching* (9th ed.). Englewood Cliffs, NJ: Prentice Hall.

Logan, P., & Skinner, C. H. (1998). Improving students' perceptions of mathematics assignments by increasing problem completion rates: Is problem completion a reinforcing event? *School Psychology Quarterly, 13,* 322–331.

Love, N. (2009). *Using data to improve learning for all: A collaborative inquiry approach.* Thousand Oaks, CA: Corwin Press.

MacQuarrie, L. L., Tucker, J. A., Burns, M. K., & Hartman, B. (2002). Comparison of retention rates using traditional drill sandwich, and incremental rehearsal flash card methods. *School Psychology Review, 31,* 584–595.

Maheady, L., Harper, G., Mallette, B., & Winstanely, N. (1991). Training and implementing requirements associate with the use of classwide peer tutoring. *Education and Treatment of Children, 14,* 177–198.

Marston, D. (1989). A curriculum-based measurement approach to assessing academic performance: What it is and why do it. In M. R. Shinn (Ed.), *Curriculum-based measurement: Assessing special children* (pp. 18–78). New York: Guilford Press

McCurdy, M., Skinner, C. H., Grantham, K., Watson, T. S., & Hindman, P. G. (2001). Increasing on-task behavior in an elementary student during mathematics seatwork by interspersing additional brief problems. *School Psychology Review, 30,* 23–32.

McCutchen, D. (1996). A capacity theory of writing: Working memory in composition. *Educational Psychology Review, 8,* 299–324.

McDonald, E., & Ardoin, S. P. (2007). Interspersing easy math problems among challenging problems: Detection of interspersal effects in whole-class applications. *Journal of Behavioral Education, 16,* 342–354.

McGlinchey, M. T., & Hixson, M. D. (2004). Using curriculum-based measurement to predict performance on state assessments in reading. *School Psychology Review, 33,* 193–203.

McMaster, K., & Espin, C. (2007). Technical features of curriculum-based measurement in writing: A literature review. *Journal of Special Education, 41,* 68–84.

McMaster, K. L., Du, X., & Petursdottir, A. (2009). Technical features of curriculum-based measures for beginning writers. *Journal of Learning Disabilities, 42,* 41–60.

McMaster, K. L., Du, X., Yeo, S., Deno, S. L., Parker, D., & Ellis, T. (2011). Curriculum-based measures of beginning writing: Technical features of the slope. *Exceptional Children, 77,* 185–206.

Meisinger, E. B., Bradley, B. A., Schwanenflugel, P. J., & Kuhn, M. (2010). Teachers' perceptions of word callers and related literacy concepts. *School Psychology Review, 39,* 54–68.

Meisinger, E. B., Bradley, B. A., Schwanenflugel, P. J., Kuhn, M., & Morris, R. (2009). Myth and reality of the word caller: The relationship between teacher nominations and prevalence among elementary school children. *School Psychology Quarterly, 24,* 147–159.

Messick, S. (1995). Validity of psychological assessment: Validation of inferences from persons' responses and performances as scientific inquiry into score meaning. *American Psychologist, 50,* 741–749.

MetaMetrics. (2013). *The Lexile framework for reading.* Available at *www.lexile.com.*

Miller, G. A. (1956). The magical number seven, plus or minus two: Some limits on our capacity for processing information. *Psychological Review, 63,* 81–97.

Miller, L. T., & Vernon, P. A. (1996). Intelligence, reaction time, and working memory in 4- to 6-year-old children. *Intelligence, 22,* 155–190.

Mosenthal, P. (1982). On designing training programs for learning disabled children: An ideological perspective. *Topical Issues in Learning Disabilities: Metacognition and Learning Disabilities, 2,* 97–107.

Moyer, S. B. (1982). Repeated reading. *Journal of Learning Disabilities, 15,* 619–623.

National Commission on Writing. (2003, April). *The neglected "R": The need for a writing revolution.* Retrieved April 1, 2013, from *www. writingcommission.org.*

National Commission on Writing. (2004). *Writing: A ticket to work . . . or a ticket out: A survey of business leaders.* Retrieved April 2, 2013, from *www.writingcommission.org/prod_downloads/ writingcom/writing-ticket-to-work.pdf.*

National Commission on Writing. (2005). *Writing: A powerful message from state government.* Retrieved April 2, 2013, from, *www. writingcommission.org/prod_downloads/writing com/powerfulmessage-from-state.pdf.*

National Council of Teachers of Mathematics. (2000). *Principles and standards for school mathematics.* Reston, VA: Author.

National Council of Teachers of Mathematics. (2006). *Curriculum focal points for prekindergarten through grade 9 mathematics: A quest for coherence.* Reston, VA: Author.

National Governors Association & Council of State School Officers. (2010). *Common Core State Standards.* Available at *www.corestandards.org.*

National Mathematics Advisory Panel. (2008). *Foundations for success: Final report of the National Math Advisory Panel.* Washington, DC: U.S. Department of Education.

National Reading Panel. (2000). *Teaching children to read: An evidence-based assessment of the scientific research literature on reading and its implications for reading instruction.* Washington, DC: National Institute of Child Health and Human Development.

Neef, N. A., Iwata, B. A., & Page, T. J. (1980). The effects of interspersal training versus high-density reinforcement on spelling acquisition and retention. *Journal of Applied Behavior Analysis, 13,* 153–158.

Nist, L., & Joseph, L. M. (2008). Effectiveness and efficiency of flashcard drill instructional methods on urban first-graders' word recognition, acquisition, maintenance, and generalization. *School Psychology Review, 37*(3), 294–308.

Northwest Evaluation Association. (2003). *Measures of academic progress for math.* Portland, OR: Author.

Northwest Evaluation Association. (2004). *Reliability and validity estimates: NWEA achievement level tests and measures of academic progress.* Lake Oswego, OR: Author.

Paris, S. G. (2002). Measuring children's reading development using leveled texts. *The Reading Teacher, 56,* 168–170.

Paris, S. G., Paris, A. H., & Carpenter, R. D. (2002). Effective practices for assessing young readers. In B. Taylor & P. D. Pearson (Eds.), *Teaching reading: Effective schools, accomplished teachers* (pp. 141–160). Mahwah, NJ: Erlbaum.

Parker, D. C., & Burns, M. K. (in press). Using the instructional level as a criterion to determine student phase of learning for reading fluency: Evidence for the learning hierarchy. *Reading and Writing Quarterly.*

Parker, D. C., Burns, M. K., & McComas, J. J. (2013). *Comparison of approaches to assess an instructional level for reading among students at-risk for reading failure.* Manuscript submitted for publication.

Parker, D. C., Burns, M. K., McMaster, K. L., & Shapiro, E. S. (2012). Extending curriculum-based assessment to early writing. *Learning Disabilities Research and Practice, 27,* 33–43.

Parker, D. C., Dickey, B. N., Burns, M. K., & McMaster, K. L. (2012). An application of brief experimental analysis with early writing. *Journal of Behavioral Education, 21,* 329–349.

Parker, D. C., McMaster, K. L., & Burns, M. K. (2011). Determining an instructional level for beginning writing skills. *School Psychology Review, 40,* 158–167.

Parker, D. C., Zaslofsky, A. F., Burns, M. K., Kanive, R., Hodgson, J., Scholin, S. E., et al. (in press).

A brief report of the diagnostic accuracy of oral reading fluency and reading inventory levels for reading failure risk among second and third grade students. *Reading and Writing Quarterly.*

Pikulski, J. J., & Chard, D. J. (2005). Fluency: Bridge between decoding and reading comprehension. *The Reading Teacher, 58,* 510–519.

Powell-Smith, K. A., & Bradley-Klug, K. L. (2001). Another look at the "C" in CBM: Does it really matter if curriculum-based measurement reading probes are curriculum-based? *Psychology in the Schools, 38,* 299–312.

Pressley, M. (2006). *Reading instruction that works: The case for balanced teaching* (3rd ed.). New York: Guilford Press.

Pressley, M., & Afflerbach, P. (1995). *Verbal protocols of reading: The nature of constructively responsive reading.* Hillsdale, NJ: Erlbaum.

Rabinowitz, M., Ornstein, P. A., Folds-Benett, T. H., & Schneider, W. (1994). Age-related differences in speed of processing: Unconfounding age and experience. *Journal of Experimental Child Psychology, 57,* 449–459.

RAND Reading Study Group. (2002). *Reading for understanding: Toward an R&D program in reading comprehension.* Santa Monica, CA & Washington, DC: RAND Corporation.

Rashotte, C. A., & Torgesen, J. K. (1985). Repeated reading and reading fluency in learning disabled children. *Reading Research Quarterly, 20,* 180–188.

Rasinski, T. V. (2003). *The fluent reader: Oral reading strategies for building word recognition, fluency, and comprehension.* New York: Scholastic.

Read Naturally. (2003). *Read Naturally master's edition teacher's manual.* St. Paul, MN: Author.

Reeve, J., Jang, H., Carrell, D., Jeon, S., & Barch, J. (2004). Enhancing students' engagement by increasing teachers' autonomy support. *Motivation and Emotion, 28,* 147–169.

Renaissance Learning. (2011). *Star math.* Wisconsin Rapids, WI: Author.

Renninger, K. A. (2000). Individual interest and its implications for understanding intrinsic motivation. In C. Sansone & J. M. Harackiewicz (Eds.), *Intrinsic and extrinsic motivation: The search for optimal motivation and performance* (pp. 373–404). San Diego, CA: Academic Press.

Reschly, A. L., Busch, T. W., Betts, J., Deno, S. L., & Long, J. D. (2009). Curriculum-based measurement oral reading as an indicator of reading achievement: A meta-analysis of the correlational evidence. *Journal of School Psychology, 47,* 427–469.

Rivera, D. M., & Bryant, B. R. (1992). Mathematics

instruction for students with special needs. *Intervention in School and Clinic, 28,* 71–86.

Roberts, M. L., Marshall, J., Nelson, J. R., & Albers, C. A. (2001). Curriculum-based assessment procedures embedded within functional behavioral assessments: Identifying escape-motivated behaviors in a general education classroom. *School Psychology Review, 30,* 264–277.

Roberts, M. L., & Shapiro, E. S. (1996). Effects of instructional ratios on students' reading performance in a regular education program. *Journal of School Psychology, 34,* 73–91.

Roberts, M. L., Turco, T. L., & Shapiro, E. S. (1991). Differential effects of fixed instructional ratios on student progress in reading. *Journal of Psychoeducational Assessment, 9,* 308–318.

Robinson, S. L., & Skinner, C. H. (2002). Interspersing additional easier items to enhance mathematics performance on subtests requiring different task demands. *School Psychology Quarterly, 17,* 191–205.

Rose, T. L. (1984). Effects of previewing on the oral reading of mainstreamed behaviorally disordered students. *Behavioral Disorders, 10,* 33–39.

Rosenfield, S., & Shinn, M. R. (1989). Another issue on curriculum-based assessment/measurement? *School Psychology Review, 18,* 297–298.

Rousseau, M. K., & Yung Tam, B. K. (1991). The efficacy of previewing and discussion of key words on the oral reading proficiency of bilingual learners with speech and language impairments. *Education and Treatment of Children, 14,* 199–209.

Saffer, N. (1999). Core subjects and your career. *Occupational Outlook Quarterly, 43*(2), 26–40.

Salahu-Din, D., Persky, H., & Miller, J. (2008). The nation's report card: Writing 2007. Retrieved March 28, 2013, from *http://nces.ed.gov/nationsreportcard/writing.*

Salvia, J. (1989). *Curriculum-based assessment: Assessing what is taught.* Upper Saddle River, NJ: Prentice Hall.

Salvia, J., Ysseldyke, J., & Bolt, S. (2007). *Assessment in special and inclusive education* (10th ed.). Boston: Houghton-Mifflin.

Salvia, J., Ysseldyke, J. E., & Bolt, S. (2010). *Assessment in special and inclusive education* (11th ed.). Belmont, CA: Wadsworth Cengage Learning.

Samuels, S. J. (1979). The method of repeated reading. *The Reading Teacher, 32,* 403–408.

Scammacca, N., Roberts, G., Vaughn, S., Edmonds, M., Wexler, J., Reutebuch, C. K., et al. (2007). *Interventions for adolescent struggling readers: A meta-analysis with implications for practice.* Portsmouth, NH: RMC Research Corporation, Center on Instruction.

Schatschneider, C., & Torgesen, J. K. (2004). Using our current understanding of cyslexia to support early identification and intervention. *Journal of Child Neurology, 19,* 759.

Schiefele, U. (1999). Interest and learning from text. *Scientific Studies of Reading, 3,* 257–279.

Scweickert, R., & Boruff, B. (1986). Short-term memory capacity: Magic number or magic spell? *Journal of Experimental Psychology: Learning, Memory, and Cognition, 12,* 419–425.

Semb, G. B., & Ellis, J. A. (1994). Knowledge taught in school: What is remembered? *Review of Educational Research, 64,* 253–286.

Shanker, J. L., & Ekwall, E. E. (2002). *Ekwall/ Shanker Reading Inventory* (5th ed.). Boston: Allyn & Bacon.

Shapiro, E. S. (1992). Use of Gickling's model of curriculum-based assessment to improve reading in elementary age students. *School Psychology Review, 21,* 168–176.

Shapiro, E. S. (2004). *Academic skills problems: Direct assessment and intervention* (3rd ed.). New York: Guilford Press.

Shapiro, E. S. (2011). *Academic skills problems: Direct assessment and intervention* (4th ed.). New York: Guilford Press.

Shapiro, E. S. (2012). *New thinking in response to intervention: A comparison of computer-adaptive tests and curriculum-based measurement within RTI.* Wisconsin Rapids, WI: Renaissance Learning.

Shapiro, E. S., & Ager, C. (1992). Assessment of special education students in regular education programs: Linking assessment to instruction. *Elementary School Journal, 92,* 283–296.

Shapiro, E. S., Angello, L. M., & Eckert, T. L. (2004). Has curriculum-based assessment become a staple of school psychology practice?: An update and extension of knowledge, use, and attitudes from 1990 to 2000. *School Psychology Review, 33,* 249–257.

Shapiro, E. S., & Gebhardt, S. N. (2012). Comparing computer-adaptive and curriculum-based measurement methods of assessment. *School Psychology Review, 41*(3), 295–305.

Shinn, M. R. (1989). *Curriculum-based measurement: Assessing special children.* New York: Guilford Press.

Shinn, M. R. (1998). *Advanced applications of curriculum-based measurement.* New York: Guilford Press.

Shinn, M. R., Rosenfield, S., & Knutson, N. (1989). Curriculum-based assessment: A comparison of models. *School Psychology Review, 18,* 299–316.

Shinn, M. R., & Shinn, M. M. (2004). *Administration*

and scoring of math curriculum-based measurement for use in general outcome measurement. Eden Prairie, MN: Edformation.

Silberglitt, B., & Hintze, J. (2005). Formative assessment using CBM-R cut scores to track progress toward success on state-mandated achievement tests: A comparison of methods. *Journal of Psychoeducational Assesment, 23,* 304–325.

Skinner, C. H., Fletcher, P. A., Wildmon, M., & Belfiore, P. J. (1996). Improving assignment preference through interspersing additional problems: Brief versus easy problems. *Journal of Behavioral Education, 6,* 427–437.

Skinner, C. H., McLaughlin, T. F., & Logan, P. (1997). Cover, copy, and compare: A self-managed academic intervention effective across skills, students, and settings. *Journal of Behavioral Education, 7,* 295–306.

Slavin, R. E. (1987). Ability grouping and student achievement in elementary schools: A best-evidence synthesis. *Review of Educational Research, 57,* 293–336.

Snow, C. E., Burns, M. S., & Griffin, P. (1998). *Preventing reading difficulties in young children.* Washington, DC: National Academies Press.

Spear-Swerling, L. (2006). Children's reading comprehension and oral reading fluency in easy text. *Reading and Writing, 19,* 199–220.

Spector, J. E. (2005). How reliable are informal reading inventories? *Psychology in the Schools, 42,* 593–603.

Speece, D. (n.d.). *How progress monitoring assists decision making in a response-to-instruction framework.* Washington, DC: National Center on Student Progress Monitoring. Available at *www. studentprogress.org/library/decisionmaking.pdf.*

Speece, D. L., & Ritchey, K. D. (2005). A longitudinal study of the development of oral reading fluency in young children at risk for reading failure. *Journal of Learning Disabilities, 38,* 387–399.

Spooner, A. L. R., Baddeley, A. D., & Gathercole, S. E. (2004). Can reading accuracy and comprehension be separated by the Neale Analysis of Reading Ability? *British Journal of Educational Psychology, 74,* 187–204.

Stage, S. A., & Jacobsen, M. D. (2001). Predicting student success on a state-mandated performance-based assessment using oral reading fluency. *School Psychology Review, 30,* 407–419.

Stanovich, K. E. (1986). Matthew effects in reading: Some consequences of individual differences in the acquisition of literacy. *Reading Research Quarterly, 21,* 360–407.

Stiggins, R. (2005). From formative assessment to assessment FOR learning: A path to success in standards-based schools. *Phi Delta Kappan, 87,* 324–328.

Szadokierski, I., & Burns, M. K. (2008). Analogue evaluation of the effects of opportunities to respond and ratios of known items within drill rehearsal of Esperanto words. *Journal of School Psychology, 46,* 593–609.

Tan, K. H., Wheldall, K., Madelaine, A., & Lee, L. W. (2009). A review of the simple view of reading: Decoding and linguistic comprehension skills of low-progress readers. *Australian Journal of Learning Disabilities, 12,* 19–30.

Therrien, W. J. (2004). Fluency and comprehension gains as a result of repeated reading: A meta-analysis. *Remedial and Special Education, 25,* 252–261.

Torgenson, J., Houston, D., & Rissman, L. (2007). *Improving literacy instruction in middle schools and high schools: A guide for principals.* Portsmouth, NH: RMC Research Cooperation, Center on Instruction.

Torgesen, J. K. (2002). The prevention of reading difficulties. *Journal of School Psychology, 40,* 7–26.

Treptow, M. A., Burns, M. K., & McComas, J. J. (2007). Reading at the frustration, instructional, and independent levels: Effects on student time on task and comprehension. *School Psychology Review, 36,* 159–166.

Tucker, J. A. (1985). Curriculum-based assessment: An introduction. *Exceptional Children, 52,* 199–204.

Tucker, J. A. (1989). *Basic flashcard technique when vocabulary is the goal.* Unpublished teaching materials, School of Education, University of Chattanooga, Chattanooga, TN.

Umbreit, J., Lane, K. L., & Dejud, C. (2004). Improving classroom behavior by modifying task difficulty. Effects of increasing the difficulty of too-easy tasks. *Journal of Positive Behavior Interventions, 6,* 13–20.

Valencia, S. W., & Riddle Buly, M. (2004). Behind test scores: What struggling readers really need. *The Reading Teacher, 57,* 520–531.

VanDerHeyden, A. M., & Burns, M. K. (2005a). Effective instruction for at-risk minority populations. In C. L. Frisby & C. R. Reynolds (Eds.), *Comprehensive handbook of multicultural school psychology* (pp. 483–516). Hoboken, NJ: Wiley.

VanDerHeyden, A. M., & Burns, M. K. (2005b). Using curriculum-based assessment and curriculum-based measurement to guide elementary mathematics instruction: Effect on individual and group accountability scores. *Assessment for Effective Intervention, 30*(3), 15–29.

VanDerHeyden, A. M., & Burns, M. K. (2009). Performance indicators in math: Implications for brief experimental analysis of academic performance. *Journal of Behavioral Education, 18,* 71–91.

VanDerHeyden, A. M., Witt, J. C., & Gilbertson, D. A. (2007). Multi-year evaluation of the effects of a response to intervention (RTI) model on identification of children for special education. *Journal of School Psychology, 45,* 225–256.

VanDerHeyden, A. M., Witt, J. C., & Naquin, G. (2003). Development and validation of a process for screening referrals to special education. *School Psychology Review, 32,* 204–227.

Vanderwood, M. L., Linklater, D., & Healy, K. (2008). Predictive accuracy of nonsense word fluency for English language learners. *School Psychology Review, 37,* 5–17.

Van de Walle, J. A., Karp, K. S., & Bay-Williams, J. M. (2010). *Elementary and middle school mathematics: Teaching developmentally* (7th ed.). Boston: Allyn & Bacon.

Van de Walle, J. A., & Lovin, L.-A. H. (2006). *Teaching student-centered mathematics: Grades K–3.* Boston: Allyn & Bacon.

Volpe, R. J., Burns, M. K., DuBois, M., & Zaslofsky, A. F. (2011). Computer-assisted tutoring: Teaching letter sounds to kindergarten students using incremental rehearsal. *Psychology in the Schools, 48,* 332–342.

Walker, R. B. (1974). *History and development of the informal reading inventory.* Unpublished manuscript.

Wayman, M. M., Wallace, T., Wiley, H. I., Ticha, R., & Espin, C. A. (2007). Literature synthesis on curriculum-based measurement in reading. *Journal of Special Education, 41,* 85–120.

William, D. (2006). Formative assessment: Getting the focus right. *Educational Assessment, 11,* 283–289.

Yeo, S. (2009). Predicting performance on state achievement tests using curriculum-based measurement in reading: A multilevel meta-analysis. *Remedial and Special Education, 31,* 1–12.

Index

Page numbers in *italic* denote a figure or table